DEAR PAULE

DEAR PAULE

HUGH LEONARD

MERCIER PRESS

MERCIER PRESS
5 French Church Street, Cork
16 Hume Street, Dublin 2

Trade enquiries to CMD DISTRIBUTION,
55a Spruce Avenue, Stillorgan Industrial Park, Blackrock, Dublin

The author and publisher are grateful to the *Sunday Independent* for permission to use material from articles originally published in the *Sunday
Independent*.

ISBN 1 85635 334 6

10 9 8 7 6 5 4 3 2 1

FOR PAULE ... OF COURSE

Printed in Ireland by Colour Books Ltd.

Preface

There are people whose entire lives are a kind of rehearsal for old age. Even when young, they adorn themselves with a *gravitas* and a surfeit of years, like a suit one has yet to grow into. There are others, and it is part of the tragi-comedy of growing old, in whom the appetite for living and gaiety remains young in an ageing body; although, under protest, they pretend to be old rather than scandalise the young. It was so with Paule and me. We stayed young and kept all the passions and insecurities of youth.

We had a switchback of a marriage, and yet our life was anchored to earth by a mooring rope of daily routine which might evolve and change with the years, but was not to be broken lest the sky would fall and the world end. For both of us on 13 April last, the sky fell and the world ended.

In later years, our daily life went in this manner. On alternate Saturdays, we would dine with our friend Max Fine at his flat in Ballsbridge; or have dinner together locally and enjoy each other's company. 'Someone is boring me,' Dylan Thomas once said, 'and I think it's me!' – well, Paule and I could infuriate each other, but boredom was never a part of it.

Sundays began with a long telephone call to our daughter Danielle, whose home was, as it still is, a flat in London, SE11. First, I myself would speak to her, then it was Paule's turn. I would drive to the village for the papers, knowing that on my return, fifteen or twenty minutes later, the pair would still be nattering. When I had made a photocopy of the *Sunday Times* crossword – we both were devotees – there was a brunch of bacon and my only permitted eggs of the week. Sunday afternoon was couch-potato time, and, in keeping with tradition, there was a roast for dinner, served either before or after Paule's favourite programme, the *Antiques Roadshow*. Strangely, in spite of my always enthusiastic intake of alcohol, it never occurred to us to drink wine at home.

On Monday evenings at 9.30 Paule went to the pub to drink coffee and finish the *Sunday Times* crossword with her friend, Eileen, and if she came home after midnight, I was lonely, self-pitying and surly. Every second Tuesday, she met the ladies whom I dubbed Coven One for an afternoon of lunch and gossip. Of an evening – again on Tuesdays and without fail – another group, Coven Two, would meet for poker until perhaps 1 a.m.

Every Thursday – a fateful day, as it proved – Paule did her shopping at Tesco in Ballybrack. She could have done so closer to home, in Dalkey, and even have had the groceries delivered, but she was Belgian, a Liegeoise, and a Walloon – and that meant that she went where the prices were lower. When she came home, the drill was that she took the grocery bags from the boot of her car, then buzzed the intercom and I went downstairs – three flights – to help her carry them up.

It was useless my telling her that we had no need to scrimp. She thought me a spendthrift. 'We are very comfortably off,' I would say, to which the reply was a crisp and knowledgeable 'No, we're not!' which closed the subject like a strong-room door. I was not allowed to get away with what might have been a boast. When I suggested that we engage a cleaning lady, she was quite implacable. 'They only make dirt,' she said. 'I'd have to follow them round, tidying up after them!'

She took pride in getting a bargain. On our one and only trip to Capri – and how I have longed to return to Axel Munthe's San Michele! – she had no sooner stepped from the funicular into the little piazza than in a boutique window she saw the same matching blouse and jacket that she had proudly bought in Dublin, except that here it was half the price. She was dismayed.

'I was rooked, at home,' she said. 'What am I going to do?'

I told her, facetiously: 'Why don't you buy it again and get it for less?'

Which was what she did, and for once extravagance was secondary. What mattered was that honour was vindicated. She had wiped out the disgrace of being over-charged. The same thing happened with a beaded handbag in a Friendship Store in Beijing; it had cost her £45 in Dublin; but in China she joyfully bought five of them at £6 each as gifts for her friends.

She had an ambivalence towards money, and it was never resolved between us. My writing, whatever she might say, had made us well-to-do, and in a corner of her mind she resented it; it was as if I had somehow put her under a compliment. 'Our money', I would say, and she would correct me with '*your* money', although we had a joint bank account. At any rate, it was a point of honour for her to spend as little as possible of 'my' money.

If we travelled Club Class by air or took a state-room with a balcony on a cruise ship or occupied the best suite in a hotel, she looked upon the comfort as a matter of course, but I suspect that in an unfocused corner of her mind she believed that another tiny fragment of her private self had been chipped away. I would stroll into hotel accommodation that had a private terrace and an ocean view and, forgetting myself, say, 'This is nice!' Whereupon she would put me in my place with a shrug and an unimpressed 'Mm'. It was as if to say that her good opinion was not for sale.

Almost every week, I had a lunch date, often with a woman friend. For company, and with a few exceptions, I have always preferred women to men; Paule knew that and kept me on a leash, a long one, but a leash for all that. If she felt me tug at it, she would have reeled it – and me – in very smartly; her territorial sense was discreet but acute.

If it was our turn to give dinner to friends, we took

them to a restaurant. Except in the most casual sense, she refused to entertain at home. As an excuse for this, she liked to cite the case of an Irish journalist and his wife who turned up at our house for dinner an hour and a half late and without apology, by which time the other guests were half-seas over and the roast of pork had shrunk to the size of a pea. The truth was that she simply hated to give dinner parties. She was a wonderful cook, but she fretted too much, worrying weeks in advance if it would be 'all right on the night'. Even when we were the guests, she had a mortal fear of arriving late. This would often result in our arriving on the dot, to be confronted by a host whose face was a mask of shaving foam and a wife caught in her slip as she fled upstairs.

We lived in a duplex on the second and third floor of an apartment building overlooking Bullock Harbour and the sea, and I worked then, as I still do, on the upper of our two floors. During the day, we gave each other a wide berth. If I needed a break or became bored with the job in hand and strayed down into her 'patch' to read or watch a film, the vacuum cleaner might suddenly come into play, to be aimed straight for my feet.

Paule was an asthmatic. There was an attack every three or four years, usually as the climax to bronchitis. An ambulance would be summoned; there was oxygen on board, and the relief was almost instantaneous. I would sit in the casualty department of St Michael's for perhaps two hours until the crisis was deemed to be over; then I was sent home, while Paule would be kept in – an impatient patient! – for perhaps 48 hours, until tests were done. Meanwhile, she bombarded me with instructions about looking after *(a)* the apartment, *(b)* the cats, The Pooka, Gladys and Panache, and *(c)* myself. Then she would come home and resume her place as the centre of our universe and all was well.

She smoked. I myself had once been a 60-a-day man; then, seventeen years ago, I kicked the habit, but too late. There was a price to pay in the currency of a triple cardiac by-pass which – the devil's children have the devil's luck – I sailed through. Paule insisted that she was only a 'social' smoker. If I suggested that she was by that criterion an intensely sociably person, she glared at me, and there was the unspoken suggestion that I was begrudging her one of her few pleasures. A few months before she died, she said: 'I'm thinking of giving up smoking.'

I said: 'Do you *want* to give them up?'

'No. No, I don't.'

'Well honestly, I'm on your side, but I would say that if you don't want to do it, then it's a lost cause. I mean, there's not much point.'

The notion of death and dying never occurred to either of us.

Every year, Danielle came home for Christmas and we set off *en famille* on the long drive to Kenmare, where we put up at the *Park Hotel* for five days. Last year, we decided to make a change. Spending an entire day in traffic from first light to beyond dusk, had something to do with it; moreover, I discovered that we could fly to Nice and stay at *La Colombe d'Or* in St Paule de Vence for less than it would cost us to spend five days on *demi-pension* at *The Park*. The public rooms at *La Colombe d'Or* were hung with pictures by Matisse, Degas, Picasso, Utrillo and Monet who had paid in kind for their room and board, and Marc Chagall was buried in the little village cemetery. Yes, it would make a change.

Well, it went wrong. Paule was never a good traveller. If a flight was delayed for merely an hour, she would say: 'This is a nightmare!' The chores of packing and unpacking would leave her exhausted, her resources spent. The more hateful a task, the more determined she was to have it over and done with. Nothing would deter her; and, in the end, the benefits of a holiday would be more than used up, so that where her strength was concerned her account went into the red.

There had been a time, when we would spend our Christmases at home in the traditional way, gorging on turkey, ham and stuffing. Friends would come visiting on the afternoon of the day itself, and there was a second, even a third, batch of them in the evening. As the night advanced, the guests tended to outstay their welcome, and Paule was too meek to proclaim a curfew and ask them, please, to go. It would not, she told me, be manners. On one particular Christmas, she was up still cleaning the apartment at five in the morning of St Stephen's Day. The result was that ten days later, she had a vicious asthma attack. When she had recovered I became all masterful and decided that thenceforth we would go away for Christmas, beyond the reach of convivial friends. And so the tradition began of going to Kenmare until, after ten years of it, we decided on the south of France.

Ireland is a lovely country until it dawns on you that it is an island off the shore of another island. To be sure of our London connection to Nice, we were obliged to get up at 5.30 a.m. on a Thursday morning. Paule had been unwilling to forfeit her Tuesday evening game of poker and had come home after 1 a.m. Wednesday was spent packing and having dinner with our friends from Ratoath who boarded the cats. She woke on the Thursday in a state of exhaustion, and by the time we reached St Paul de Vence, bronchitis had set in.

I put her to bed at once in our suite, which – a small mercy – was spacious, with a glimpse of willows and pines, and at least the climate was bone-dry. I had food sent up from the hotel restaurant: first, soup, then boiled fish. After two days, Paule was out of bed and the three of us spent Christmas Day at the new home of our friends, Peter and Alicia White, two miles away. It was a happy day, with good food and stories, and Paule was back in form and not overdoing it. Next day, we took a bus into Nice and had lunch at one of the little fish restaurants by the Old Port.

Her luck, however, was still out and with a vengeance. There was a storm, and the aircraft that was to take us from Nice to Heathrow had been damaged. In its time-hallowed way, the 'World's Favourite Airline' treated us like cattle; after four hours of excuses and outright lies, we were taken to a Holiday Inn and put up for the night. When we did take off the following morning, Paule was alarmingly ill. She seemed to recover, but I only now suspect that the real damage had been done.

We had made plans for other journeys this year. In July we were to cruise on yet another French canal, this one in Alsace, but it held no fears for Paule as we were to get there by car, with most of the luggage stowed any-which-way in garment bags instead of tidily packed in cases. And for Christmas we were to go by ferry and again by car to the Isle of Eriska, a Scottish hotel on a lovely island one reached across a rusting iron bridge. We had been there twice and loved it.

In early April, I finished my first novel, *A Wild People,* and on the twelfth I gave the typescript to Paule. It amounted to 240 pages, and I suggested that she read sixty pages every night – she enjoyed reading in bed. Next morning, I asked her 'Well?'

She laughed and nodded and said, 'I love it. It's very funny!'

That afternoon, she did her weekly shopping as usual. I had been plagued by back pains throughout the winter and what passes for an Irish springtime – these had been variously diagnosed as sciatica, lumbago, disc trouble, old age and all of these together; so she had stopped ringing the doorbell as a signal for me to come down and help her with the bags. The first I knew that she was home was the sound of our hall door slamming behind her when the shopping had been lugged upstairs.

'Will you please ring the bloody bell!' I would snarl, rushing down to the kitchen, and the answer was a shrug.

On this 13 April, she came home tired out and after a while asked if I would mind having dinner on my own at a restaurant in the village. This was unusual; I had often suggested that I eat out to save her the chore of cooking, and she refused to hear of such a thing; now, however, she was actually suggesting it. Well, there was a first time for everything, and I still could discern no hint that she was unwell. At six o'clock I went to my local for a drink, then had a plate of spaghetti and a glass of wine at the trattoria next door. On my return, Paule said: 'I fed the cats, and it sent me back to square one.' It did occur to me that doling out cat food into three dishes should not have called for much in the way of exertion.

She went into the bedroom, next door to the living-room, and sat on the coverlet. I watched television, and after a time she appeared, undressed, in the doorway and asked if I would take her to hospital.

I said: 'Is it an asthma attack?'

She said: 'I don't know.'

Usually, in her case, asthma did not come out of the blue; it was an accompaniment to an onset of bronchitis or a respiratory crisis. I helped her to put on a beige-coloured woollen top; then she said, 'get an ambulance. It'll be quicker.'

I telephoned and was told that the paramedics would be with us within minutes. When I returned to the bedroom, she was no longer there. I found her in the living-room, kneeling by the glass door that opened on to the terrace that looked out on the bay and across to Howth. There was a cold wind from the sea, and she was gasping for air. I put my hands on her shoulders from behind and begged her to hold on. She reached up and pushed my hands away. At the same moment, I looked down at her face and saw that her eyes were half-open, an unblinking clouded blue. I knew then that she was gone.

The paramedics came, as did our next-door neighbour. I called Danielle in London and our friend, Max, in Ballsbridge. By then, the paramedics had left, taking Paule with them. Later – time was meaningless – the hospital called to confirm that she was dead and to say that since it had happened at home and without the attendance of a doctor, I would have to identify the body. Max drove me to the hospital where two policemen were waiting. Paule seemed peaceful, as if she had merely closed her eyes, but there was a red line across the soft flesh above the bridge of her nose. I asked if the paramedics had perhaps caused this with their breathing apparatus. The hospital doctor denied it most defensively. It was strange; near the end of my novel there is a farcical accident, when the narrator's wife, Greta, accidentally drives her car over a seaside groyne, and her spectacles cut into the fleshy part of her nose just above the bridge.

Another thing was Paule's final gesture in pushing my hands away from her shoulders. Was it because I was impeding her breathing, or could it have been a rejection? In shock, all reason breaks down, and, on top of all else, both mysteries stayed to haunt me in what was perhaps a kind of madness. They still do, and this is terrible to write.

It occurred to me that Paule would not have wanted a religious service, and yet neither would she have denied her friends a chance to say goodbye. I decided to call on the Rev. Martin Murnaghan of Dalkey, but my thought was father to his deed, and he rang me virtually at that instant. Things happened. The President called and offered condolences. Two cousins, Gaston and Josette, and Danielle's godson, Xavier, came from Belgium. A weekend passed in a haze of shock and pain, and out of it only one thought came clearly, and it was that I wanted to follow Paule. There are moments, many months later, when I still do. There are unfinished conversations and unspoken words that will not keep.

The morning of the funeral was warm and sunny. As Danielle and I entered the crowded chapel yard, I said to her: 'Remember that Mum is not in that box in front of the altar.' There is a proverb that says: 'More people know Tom Fool than Tom Fool knows'; and I knew that many who were no more than morbidly curious would be in the church, avid to see pain. Dan and I managed to keep tears at bay; in fact, as we walked down the centre aisle, she said, corner of her mouth, 'G– and B– are here.'

(G– and B–, who were once close friends, were an admirable, good-living couple who had been through what they saw as a family crisis. When it had passed, they hunted it entirely from their memory. As far as they were concerned, it had simply never happened, and Paule and I, who had been unwillingly pressed into service as comforters, were banished, too. The couple had not spoken to us in fifteen years. Even today, while B– signed the attendance book in the church porch, her husband G– did not).

The service was as moving as any I can recall or perhaps this was the first time I had ever listened. From the same altar where, as a boy, I had heard priests fulminate and threaten their listeners with hellfire and eternal roasting, Father Murnaghan spoke of God's love and mercy in what for our town was so heretical a manner as to steer me back towards a faith I still only half believed in.

In fact, I was so distraught that I prayed for the first time in years and asked God to allow me to take upon myself the small burden of Paule's sins. Later, when Father Murnaghan called to the apartment, I asked him if this had been a permissible request. He said it was. (It occurs to me that, if he did not really think so, he probably thought of it as a good idea!) Then I heard myself saying, and no smart aleckry was intended: 'Well, if I now have her sins as well as my own, would you please give me absolution?' After sixty years I was back in the good graces of a God I badly needed to believe in, and I heard the words: 'And now, for your penance remember her.'

It was not a penance as much as a life sentence, and as Basil Hume said: 'To try to pray is in itself prayer.'

In the days after the funeral, Dan and I set about the wretched business of disposing of Paule's clothes and the shoes that were her one extravagance. For me, the shock of her death – 45 years wiped away in a few minutes – obscured the natural grief that was awaiting its turn, and there were born two kinds of aloneness, one emotional, the other to do with the prosaic business of staying alive. As an adopted child, I had lived with my foster-parents for 28 years, and then Paule took over. Now and for the first time, I would be alone. That seemed unimportant, and it still does, for it is made trivial by Paule's absence.

During the first week, I wanted at all costs to talk to her. If I attempted to do this in my mind, the result was tears, an uncontrollable collapse into weeping. So I utilised the discipline of writing and that was the first of the *Dear Paule* letters. When I wrote my play, *Da*, 27 years ago, the effort of remembering my father, of selecting, of putting the right words into the right order, of being conscious that there would be an audience to look on and listen – all of this, the business of being a writer, kept tears at bay.

I had no sentimental fancy that there was in any sense an angel on my shoulder or that, as some readers have assured me, Paule was reading that first letter. I do believe in continuity, in survival after death, and it is not because I want to, but because to me it makes sense. In Thornton Wilder's great play, *Our Town*, the Stage Manager/Chorus says:

> Now there are some things we all know, but we don't take'm out and look at very often. We all know that *something* is eternal. And it ain't houses and it ain't names, and it ain't earth and it ain't even the stars. Everybody knows in their bones that *something* is eternal, and that something has to do with human beings. All the greatest people ever lived have been telling us that for five thousand years and yet you'd be sur-

prised how people are always losing hold of it. There's something way down deep that's eternal about every *human being*.

I believe this; in fact, I *know* it whenever I see a painting by Rembrandt or Monet or Van Gogh or an L. S. Lowry matchstick man; or when I look at Chartres Cathedral from eight miles away across the wheat fields or the Parthenon rearing white above the blue smog of Athens with the Aegean behind; or when I hear Beethoven, or the words of Shakespeare, or even a play by Samuel Beckett – which must cause merriment in heaven, for by the genius of his writing he disproves the nothingness he would have us believe in.

I do not know in what form or how Paule survives, but I know with certainty that her essence does live on. The universe wastes nothing. Perhaps, like the hero of J. B. Priestley's play, *Johnson over Jordan*, her soul will set out on a lonely star-journey from the Inn at the World's End. I fear, in spite of many of the hundreds of people who wrote to me, that I have seen the last of her. If not, it would be a nice surprise! And I doubt that she was on a cloud reading that first letter of mine; which in any case was really written to myself, to ease the pain and make it seem as if Paule were no further away than the next room.

Why I chose to e-mail it to the *Sunday Independent* for publication I had no idea. I felt vaguely guilty about it. Then a tall stranger a man who, I swear, had but one leg came hopping after me on the street and, as if he had read my thoughts, said 'Well done, sir! If you had been a painter and made a portrait of your wife, surely you would have found a place for it on a wall and hung it there. If you were a composer and wrote a piece of music in her memory, you would have played it. Instead, you have written her a letter, so why shouldn't you publish it?'

The 'Dear Paule' letters are not intended to be a kind of biography or a record of a marriage; rather they are a record of my coping or failing to cope with the early days of bereavement. Paule was always far too private a person to endure having her life sold over a bookshop counter. I recall that one of her favourite films was the comedy, *Moonstruck,* and her best-loved scene was when the Italian-American mother (Olympia Dukakis) suddenly says to her philandering husband across the family table: 'I want you to stop seeing her!' Paule almost applauded at that moment, and yet she herself would have been too proud for any kind of confrontation; her dignity would not have allowed it. Rather, she would have nursed her hurt and perhaps sublimated her grievance in bouts of in-fighting.

Many of my correspondents have created their own mythology about Paule and me. By insisting that ours was a marriage made in heaven, they mistake love for happiness. Because I loved Paule and, as I believe, she loved me, they assume that our marriage was unfailingly happy. It was not. It endured for nearly 45 years and went through many phases. For much of the time, I made her miserable, and she was quick to repay. Often, I took my vows too lightly, whereas Paule – strange for a good sailor! – was too inflexible to roll with the sea.

People, especially women, nowadays declare that they want their own 'space'. It is an overworked phrase, but still a useful one. It means elbow-room in which one can be one's own untrammelled self within a relation-ship. Paule was not familiar with the expression, other-wise I know that she would have used it unmercifully. Often, if we had a quarrel, the root of it was that she felt her 'space' to be threatened, although I would contend that it never was.

Once, not long ago, we met a man whom the police suspected of being a murderer. For want of evidence, there had been no arrest, and the man turned out to be amicable, jolly and the best of good company. Butter, as they say, wouldn't melt. Next morning, I poked my head into our bathroom, and a small comedy ensued. I said: 'You're a peculiar woman.'

She asked, 'How?'

'We spent all last evening with that man, and yet you've said nothing whatever about him. I mean, you've uttered not a word about whether you thought him innocent or guilty. That's not like you at all.'

She was silent for a moment, then: 'I said nothing

because you'd only make a jeer of my opinion, like you always do.'

I was hurt. I said, and it was true, that I had never jeered at her in my life. She did not reply. Then I said: 'Well, if you want *my* opinion, I think he's as guilty as hell.'

She smiled, and it was as if the sun had come out. She said, 'Oh, so do I!'

I cherished the irony, that for us to be lovingly at one with each other was more important to Paule than whether or not a suburban Othello had throttled his wife. Even so, I recognised an old grievance dressed in new clothes; not for the first time, she was defending a stronghold that had never been under attack.

No, our relationship was always prickly, much to the amusement of our friends, who knew the depth of the underlying affection. And I have seen Paule go to my defence with sabre teeth. I have mentioned our one-time friends, G– and his wife B–, who came to the funeral. G– found a feeble and even risible pretext for ending our 30-year friendship; it was a trumped up excuse that was a light-year from the reality. Paule, however, continued to go shopping with B– every week, and I encouraged her, nursing the hope that as long as they stayed friends there was hope that G– and I might reconcile. One day, Paule urged B– to see a play of mine before its run ended.

'G– and I have no intention of going,' B– said. 'And

if I were you, I would disown the kind of things he writes.' She was referring, not to my plays, but my Sunday column.

'In that case, B–,' Paule said with equal politeness, 'I won't come shopping with you next week.'

And that was the end of that. And now I have lost not only a best friend and lover but also a protector who was both critic and champion.

A calmness that had little to do with age overtook us during the last several years. To resort to cliché, it was as if we had forsaken the high seas with its storms and perils for a sheltered inlet, although there were still occasions when I would go stomping the half-mile to the village with a head full of grievances, mentally rehearsing the mother and father of all confrontations. It was an Armageddon that would never have come, for the tragedy is that we were coming to a new and affectionate rapport. Anyway, where quarrelling is concerned, I am a bad fighter; I lose interest; I too quickly go off the boil and sue for peace; Paule, on the other hand, would enjoy fighting to the last ditch, never yielding ground or turning tail. It was as if her soul were under threat.

The 'Dear Paule' letters attracted much interest. With misgivings on my part – unfounded, as it transpired – I was interviewed on the Marian Finucane radio show, and she asked me if I was bothered that the letters might attract voyeurs. There are always those who need to see pain and will run to, instead of from, a road accident; well, that, as the saying goes, was their problem. I was more interested in my correspondents, many of whom were themselves bereaved. Some had lost a partner as long as thirty or forty years before, and still mourned. Some went in dread of a future bereavement, with themselves, like me, as the survivor.

Many people gave advice, all of it useless because there was no known cure for what ailed me. At first, I lived from day to day, then, when the pain eased, from week to week. The shock passed, and grief took its place. I could not look up at a clear night sky without lamenting that Paule had been denied it, or see a film without wanting to share it. I watched the episode of our favourite show, *Frasier*, in which at long last Niles and Daphne ran off together, and I could almost see Paule, beside me on the sofa, give a smile of pure pleasure at the end. She was wherever I looked, in a ceramic cat I bought her in Joigny, in the potted plants she tended so lovingly, and even in the fine-comb and brush with which she groomed our long-haired Balinese, Panache.

People wrote to say they knew how I felt, although they could not possibly, for they were not I, nor had they lost Paule. A few know-alls told me how long my grieving would last: a year, five years, forever. The widow of a dear friend of ours who had died two years before, said, dryly: 'Now you'll know what it's like.' A nun told me sternly that writing the 'letters to Paule' was useless, that what she was in need of were my prayers. Others insisted that Paule was watching over me, and in a sense, I felt this to be true, but 'watching' and 'helping' were a long way apart. People sent letters and cards to say that I was coping 'brilliantly', although all they could see – and all they were meant to see – was a face put on, like an overcoat, for out of doors.

I wrote fourteen letters to Paule, then called a halt. Even an hour ago, as I write these words, two people stopped me on the street, each to say that the letters had been of help in a private grief. One of them asked why I had stopped, and I gave him the glib non-answer 'Enough is enough.'

The truth, however, was that I was not fulfilling my penance: 'Remember her'.

The letters were addressed to a Paule who – in a very real sense, to me, at any rate – was immediate and still living; and on that account there was no past tense and nothing to be remembered. I knew that I could not begin to climb out of the abyss until I put her behind me, in what no longer was the present. I have not ceased to love her. She is in this room with me. Nothing has changed, except that for the first time I have had to face up to it – that she is gone. 'Dead', I suppose, is the word I seek. An American would say 'passed away' or even 'passed over', as if death were a rope bridge or the ocean liner in *Outward Bound*.

In fact, the mention of a rope bridge puts another metaphor into my mind. Now that I no longer have the letters as a crutch to help me limp along, perhaps one day I can exclaim: 'Look, no hands!'

1

My dearest Paule,

As all the tributes and kind words came flooding in, I thought of Dame Sybil Thorndyke, who was married for many years to Sir Lewis Casson. A reporter asked her if either of them had ever contemplated divorce, and her reply was: 'Murder, frequently; divorce, never!' So it was with us.

You would hate it if I were to write about what you would call 'love and stuff'. Do you, however, remember a morning about three weeks ago – in what for you is now another world? You had summoned me down from my workroom to have breakfast, and I made some small joke at your expense, whereupon you burst out laughing and said: 'Oh, you pig!'

Being called a pig is not an everyday kind of endearment, but I had to leave the kitchen for a moment to conceal my happiness. I had always been sure of your love, even in the midst of the worst of door-slamming and not-talking rows; now I knew that you liked me as well. Good, fine, splendid, as the fellow said in

Peg o' My Heart, and with that the gush is over with.

It is a week today since you jumped the queue, usurping my place in it and sneaking off, as quietly as a cloud passing over the face of the sun; which is a bad simile, since this cloud is one that won't pass. It has been a week of sheer hell, and the cloud gets darker.

A dear friend of mine, offering comforting words, has said that I took you to many places you would otherwise have never seen and introduced you to people you would otherwise never have met. I could have told her that you hated to travel, and, apart from those friends we had deeply in common – Max, Melinda, Margaret and Joe, Julia and Ciaran and Bernard and Gloria, for instance – you always preferred the company of the nice ladies whom I jokingly dubbed 'Coven One' and 'Coven Two'.

I secretly suspect that they believed I wasn't good enough for you. Well, who is arguing? Not I, for sure. You married a stony-broke civil servant who turned into a playwright. You didn't complain, but I had the impression of a woman who had gone into a restaurant and ordered rice pudding, only to be served with, say, apple charlotte. It was very nice and all that – you would eat anything, the simpler the better – but it was not quite what you had ordered.

Nonetheless, you chortled with pleasure last week on reading the first four chapters of my book – I had rationed you to four daily 60-page helpings. You never read further than the first 60.

At this moment, I should be downstairs getting something to eat to keep from falling over, or helping Danielle to throw out dust-gathering ornaments, or putting things to one side for Oxfam; but I want to talk to you for a while.

Thousands – millions, rather – of people go through this grief: at a time when one heart stops and another breaks. There is the sheer paralysing inability to get out of bed, to dress, wash, eat, or to face the empty space at the table.

Our tortoiseshell, Gladys, comes kneading at your pillow – minx that she is, she always slept in the crook of your neck – whereas The Pooka, who is 'my' cat, comes unbidden and puts his face against mine. The worst part of it all is a future with nothing in it. For the present and maybe 10 times a day, I think, 'Oh, I must tell Paule about this', and then I remember what 'alone' is.

Much as you were always unimpressed by any show of pomp or importance, you would have been touched as I was when the President phoned and followed this up with an affectionate handwritten letter saying that a special mass would be celebrated next week at the Aras. The letter was signed 'Mary', and what a great and good girl she is.

Also, there was the endless kindness of Father Murnaghan of Dalkey, who was, as Danielle – who is not a believer – said, a 'star'. Myself, I remain a half-believer.

What I did was not in any sense a road-to-Damascus kind of conversion, but in the abyss of my despair I turned to one who for me has always been a very murky kind of God. From Father Murnaghan I heard about love and not judgement, and he spoke the words: 'And for your penance – remember her.' Easy-peasy, and I think I can hear you laugh.

Well, you should have been at that funeral – and, of course, you weren't. As the saying goes, you missed it. Dan and I managed not to break down; I told her to remember that it was not you in the box. Father Murnaghan gave a homily that nearly quite undid my resolve; our kindly neighbour Stella Teehan read the lesson, and our friend, Max Fine, struck a blow for ecumenism by delivering the eulogy – you would have enjoyed this last!

And there were mates from my Land Commission days – you would have gossiped their ears off the whole day long; I can hear your joyous rediscovering cry of 'Roisin!', 'Bridie!', 'Aideen!' and 'Mary!' There were people from the *Indo* and the Abbey, as well as one (better than none at all, and thank you, Marie) from the Gate.

My oldest friend, Mark Grantham, who would win a gold in the Curmudgeon Olympics, came from Paris. And you would have been especially pleased to espy a couple who have been black out with us for years. Alas, she signed the attendance book, and he did not.

That hurt.

This evening, Dan and I will play one of your best-loved films, *The Shop Around the Corner*. Another favourite – you could not see it too often – was *Moonstruck*, and I am sorry that my nerve failed and, as the coffin left the church, there was an aria from *La Rondine* instead of Dean Martin belting out 'That's Amore'.

This winter I was crippled with a mixture of lumbago and sciatica, and I suggested to you that the real culprit was winter itself. Lucky were they, I said, who lived in the south of France.

At once you went on the attack, just in case I got any queer notions. You worked far too hard – it killed you, I think – ever to be a couch potato, but you would not dream of putting yourself outside the range of *Heartbeat*, *Last of the Summer Wine*, *The Antiques Roadshow* and *A Touch of Frost*. Not to mention poker on Tuesdays and cryptic crosswords at any time – no more will I use the fax machine to make copies of Crossaire and the *Sunday Times*.

I had begged you over and over again to get a cleaning woman, saying we could well afford it, but with a mixture of pride and Belgian frugality, you said no, there was none who was ever caring enough. So you polished silver and humped bags and invited that last dreadful asthma attack.

Danielle is drawing up lists and giving me lessons in using the washing machine, and my godmother,

Helen Lucy Burke, is on the trail of a lady who will 'do' for me; else I shall go native. It all seems singularly pointless, and there are probably readers who will say that in writing this I am putting a private grief on public show. Not so; it is the effort of putting feelings into words and words into sentences that keeps tears – howls of grief, rather – at bay. I write, because writing is what I do.

And I am mawkish enough to think of you now, sitting among all the mogs of our life in Elysium, every one of them purring like mad while you tell dirty jokes to the saints. And what a laugh you had! I think, all of a sudden of William Blake:

> Man was made for Joy and Woe
> And when this we rightly know,
> Thro' the world we safely go.
> Joy and Woe are woven fine,
> A clothing for the soul divine.

Alas, I hadn't prepared myself for nearly so much woe, but as the girl said in one of your favourite jokes, keep an eye out for me.

Love, and then some,
Jack

2

Dear Paule,

So ask me how do I feel.

'How do you feel?'

Don't ask.

Among your favourite European cities were London and Barcelona, but for some reason, now lost in the mists of the great feminine 'Because', you always loathed Paris. And so we went there only once in our nearly 45 years and neither Notre Dame and the Seine and *bateaux mouches* at night, nor the street musician who cajoled us into singing 'La Valse Brune' could melt your profound antipathy. (I suspect that if you ask a woman why she does not like a particular thing, she will truthfully reply: 'Because I disliked it yesterday.')

Well, I have decided that once Danielle has returned to London and I have dipped my spoon into alone-ness for a few days, I shall go to Paris, find a hotel on the Ile Saint Louis, revisit the post-Impressionists, and take my fellow-curmudgeon, Mark Grantham, to dinner at *Le Vieux Bistro* in the shadow of the cathedral.

I hear you saying 'Well, don't ask me to go with

you!' but I'll be taking you along anyway.

Friday
A favourite story of yours concerned a time when you were ill with a bout of asthma and had not eaten for several days. Then, feeling yourself to be on the mend, you declared that you wouldn't mind a cup of soup. (The phrase 'wouldn't mind' was the nearest you ever came to saying 'I want'. Once, when we had viewed a Dalkey apartment that overlooked the sea, you said, rather shyly: 'I wouldn't mind living there', and in consequence that was where you died, sixteen years later.)

Anyway, I galloped to the kitchen and combined a tin of Heinz and a tin of Campbells with a flourish worthy of Escoffier. The trouble was that I could not find the master-switch for the hot-plate of our cooker. If I were to consult you on the matter, you would have sighed, got wearily out of bed – with me yelling 'Just tell me!' – and done the whole thing yourself, wheezing about the uselessness of men in general and me in particular. So I made the soup in the electric kettle. You actually took a swig and gasped, 'it's lovely!'

Then, as weeks passed, you realised the truth and went demented in your futile attempts to spear the peas and bits of carrot that were stuck fast under the element of the kettle. Eventually, tired of drinking turnip-flavoured Lyons Green Label and Maxwell House with onions in it, we consigned the samovar to the bin.

The story entered into family mythology; someone even told it last Tuesday at the funeral.

This, for you, was the final, devastating proof of my hopelessness. When it came to making beds, using a washing machine, mending a hole in a sock and feeding the cats, I would yell: 'Just teach me!' You would shake your head as if I had asked you for a splinter from the True Cross. Absurdly, I could hear the final lisping words of Boris Karloff as an expiring mad scientist: 'There are some things that it is best for man not to know.'

At any rate, today Danielle and I interviewed and were interviewed by the lady Ms Mopp who, one hopes, is to 'do' for me from now on. Meanwhile, friends keep telephoning and e-mailing with offers of help, and of course no help is possible. In my present mood, I think of Dorothy Parker's:

> Guns aren't lawful;
> Nooses give;
> Gas smells awful:
> You might as well live.

And a fat lot she knew about it. Or to use that tasteless Crucifixion tagline: 'This is *Good* Friday?'

Saturday
In town this afternoon a nosy acquaintance asked if I had received a message of sympathy from an avowed friend, who is also a famous broadcaster. I told the lady

that the world is divided into two kinds of people: those who send messages of affection, and those who instead sit back and wait to receive them. A bit like God, come to think of it.

And there is no word from our one-time intimate, the Gate-keeper, either. Paule dearest, do I hear you weep? No, thought not.

This afternoon. Danielle set off to go into town and meet a chum, but because of repair work to bridges, there was no DART service between Bray and Dun Laoghaire. So Dan became one of a small aggrieved band of would-be travellers at Dalkey station, where a minion said that today's spanner in the works or work on the spanners, perhaps, had been well advertised.

'But there is no notice here, at this railway station,' Dan said.

The minion shrugged.

She asked: 'Is there a feeder bus service?'

'Oh, yeah, there's one o' dem.'

'At what intervals?'

'Dunno.' Then, brightly: 'But one is juss-now gone.'

So the passengers quitted this forlorn outpost of the West Clare Railway and slogged to the CIE bus stop at the other end of the town, and there, sure enough, was a waiting double-decker. There were smiles, pre-mature as it proved. 'When is it due to depart?' the travellers asked.

'In 25 minutes,' they were told.

Life goes on. Or, rather, it doesn't.

Easter Sunday
Thanks to my godmother, Helen Lucy Burke, we were invited for lunch at a gorgeous Queen Anne mansion in Wicklow. Apart from our host, there were charming teenagers and a group of delightful people. The sun shines, and it could have been an idyllic scene from *A Room with a View* or *Une Partie de Campagne*. And, perhaps as a reaction to the horrors of the past two weeks I went on a 'high' and, like Yorick, set the table on a roar with well-worn stories about Anew McMaster, John Gielgud and Molly Keane.

And, of course, there was an emotional comeuppance or, rather, a come-down as soon as I had returned home, for I learnt that the higher one flies, the more devastating the crash afterwards. God forgive me, I honestly never realised that I loved you that much.

Monday
I lie in bed, not wanting to get up, ever. Living has now become like the *Late Late Show*; inasmuch as the only reason one does not pull the plug is the irrational hope that the next segment will be tolerable. It so rarely is. And today I have a sore throat. Dan says that out of shock and grief I have succumbed to what is called immune deficiency. Well, Paule, here's another nice mess you've gotten me into.

Meanwhile, Easter bank holiday and all as it is, Ms Mopp has arrived for her first stint and, as I write, is whirring like a combine harvester. Danielle whispers to me with what approaches awe: 'Dad, she's dusting *under* the ornaments!' How often did I beg you, Paule, to find a cleaning woman, and the reply was always that she would skimp the job? 'All they ever do is create work.'

Besides which, we were an odd couple. I spent money like a drunken sailor – back in 1963, with a total of £2,000 in the bank, I went to London and splashed out £1,200 of it on a Lowry painting of factory chimneys and matchstick people. You, on the other hand, had true Belgian frugality and were hard on yourself. 'Your trouble,' you would tell me severely, 'is that you think we are well off!'

After four hours, our apartment is a new pin, and as Ms Mopp departs, I say to Dan: 'Guess what that woman's first action would be if she ever became rich?'

'She'd get herself a cleaning woman,' Dan says.

'Right!'

Tuesday

There are scores nay, hundreds, of letters and cards. I never knew nor did you how well and widely loved you were, not as an adjunct of a Tom-Fool writer but on your own account. And, alas, there is mail of another kind.

As you know, for more than two months now some gnat-brained hoaxer has been sending away for holiday brochures and using my name. Every resort town and village in these islands has replied, flooding the house with junk mail, which you, Lord love you, had to dispose of. The blackguard has even forged my signature to take out subscriptions to *Time, Newsweek* and other magazines.

Today, there are brochures and videotapes from children's summer camps across America. I daresay he has been playing with that electronic yo-yo, the Internet. Paule, if you can find time in your new abode, would you mind singling him out and sending down a small, gobshite-seeking thunderbolt? Ta.

This afternoon, it is time for Dan to return to London, and as I drive her to the airport I tell her about a certain Italian woman, an acquaintance of mine who is, to put it kindly, a weaver of many fantasies. She once told me that her husband had received an anonymous letter concerning myself and asked what she should do about it. Privately wondering if such a letter even existed, I told her to tear it up and, by the way, invited her to lunch.

Her car and mine arrived together at the restaurant, and at once she waved a small piece of paper at me. 'This is the letter.'

I said: 'You didn't take my advice, then?'

She said, rather indignantly: 'I did exactly what

you said. I tore it up, but first I made a copy!'

Dan laughed so helplessly at this that we nearly hit a lorry at Fairview. It reminded me that you, she and I had different tastes in many things: in music, art and books, for example, but an identical, raucous, bawdy, punning, Wodehousian sense of humour was the glue that bound the three of us most tightly together.

She has been a rock over these twelve days, but at the airport she wept. I had time to say: 'Your mother did a good job on you' before myself caving in as she said, 'And on you'.

And now, my dear Paule, I must leave you and love you and go and feed the mogs.

Love,
Jack

3

Wednesday

Dear Paule,

Last evening I scalded both my hands because I had forgotten to switch off the hot water. Then, in the early hours, I woke up in a dripping sweat; in fact, even the mogs were perspiring, and all because I had omitted to turn off the central heating. This morning, I opened a cupboard to find a plate, and the door fell off.

There is something irresistibly funny about a clumsy male blundering about in what is traditionally a female domain. His wife is either in hospital or away visiting a relative, and he spends his time walking backwards so that he can clean his spoor as he goes. And while I have an almost non-existent sense of smell, yours more than made up for it.

I always half-dreaded your return from, say, visiting cousins in Liege. On the day before your homecoming, I would work myself daft opening windows, vacuuming and scrubbing the sink, but it was in vain. You had only to walk in the door after a week's absence, and you were reeling and emitting near-operatic cries of 'Faugh!' and 'Phew!' followed by a few fervent 'Yecchs!' which I think you had rehearsed on the plane. And I would slink up to my workroom, muttering 'I hate her!' under my breath.

Well, you aren't ever going to walk in the door again, and in the meantime the cards and messages are still coming. So far there are, at a guess, going on for three hundred of them, more than I can ever hope to reply to personally. All words of counsel are useless; the most comforting of them advise me to give thanks that you was spared what I am now going through. Well, that at least makes sense. A tough guy, in an e-mail, tells me, like Duke Wayne admonishing a tenderfoot: 'Get back in the saddle.' Gobshite.

I recall that seven years ago when I underwent a triple cardiac by-pass, I asked a friend to have some flowers delivered to you on my behalf on the morning of the operation. That was not as sadistic as it may seem, for I wanted you to have a just-in-case message which was enclosed with the bouquet. A couple of years later, I found the letter, apparently grease-stained, in the kitchen at home.

Rather aggrieved, I asked you either to tear it up or put it away, out of sight of prying eyes. I don't know what you did with it, and I pray that I shall never come across it, for only later did it dawn on me that what I took to be spots of grease were actually tear-stains.

Many of the letters of comfort tell me that one day we, you and I that is, will meet again. That would be nice if it were true, but an irreverent thought occurs to me. Supposing a man or a woman has more than one spouse, how are matters ordered in the hereafter? Does the Almighty put them on a kind of rota? – Mary on Monday, Wednesday and Friday, and Madge on Tuesday, Thursday and Saturday, with Sundays to be spent re-stringing one's harp.

There was a time when I used to refer to you, waggishly, as my 'present wife'. You took it in good part, even when the joke wore thin; then you learned that a certain lady – in Waterford, I think – was declaring as an irrefutable fact that you were my Mate No. 3. So I abandoned the silliness, but the tag endures.

This evening, my dear friend Pat Donlon gave me a precious hour of comfort as well as a splendid dinner, and I told her a story you related to me during our courting days. You warned me that you would deny it, which you certainly did!, if I told another soul. Well, you can't deny it now.

Both your father and uncle Edouard were in the Belgian diplomatic service, and during the Second World War they were both stationed at the embassy in Moscow. When the Germans advanced to within 30 miles of the city, you, with your mother and aunt were sent eastwards by the trans-Siberian railway to Vladivostok and by ship from there to Los Angeles. There you lived out the war and learned English.

(You were born left-handed, but your father would have none of such nonsense and trained you to favour

your right hand like 'normal' folk. It was in consequence of this, or so a psychologist once told me, that
your brain had a 'crossover' pattern, so that you con-
cocted spoonerisms. Once, while watching a film about
the RAF, you asked me: 'Are those the men who dam-
med the busts?' And, while cruising the Vilaine river in
Brittany, you consulted a map and told me that we
were twenty miles from Redon, 'as the fly crows'.)

By 1944, the German threat had receded, and your
father and uncle were transferred from Moscow to the
embassy at Bombay. Meanwhile, an MGM talent scout
visited your school and auditioned several girls for a
starring role in a film soon to be made. The choice nar-
rowed down to either you or a certain teenage actress,
a year younger than you, who was already under con-
tract to the studio. A screen test was ordered, and your
mother cabled your father in India for his permission.

He refused, replying that he had no wish to see his
only child become a spoiled film star brat. You had no
acting ambitions and were not in the least perturbed,
so the role went by default to the other girl. The film,
as it happened, was *National Velvet*.

Another story, one which you told eagerly, is that a
year or so later, when you went to rejoin your father in
India, you travelled by sea via Australia. There, a dock-
ers' strike caused you and and your mother and aunt
to miss an onward connection from Sydney to Bombay. The vessel you should have taken set sail on the

thirteenth of the month and disappeared with all on board in a typhoon in the Indian Ocean. Ever since then, you staunchly regarded thirteen as your lucky number.

[Paule died on 13 April.]

Thursday

I find myself remembering Norman Rodway. He and I were very great for a time, although you never liked him much – he was a 'luvvy' before the word came into vogue, and you always detested being addressed as 'Dahhhling'. Anyway, he starred in a Joyce adaptation of mine called *Stephen D.* and took London by storm. Kenneth Tynan wrote of him: 'Hereafter, Finney had better look to his laurels and O'Toole to his Lawrence'. All Rodway's notices were unqualified raves except one. The *Economist* referred to him as 'one of Ireland's more charmless sons'.

And, of course, that was the review he took to be his proper deserts – all the panegyrics and hosannas went for nothing. Which, I suppose, is human nature. Perhaps we all suspect that deep down we are ne'er-do-wells, like Dylan Thomas' 'No-Good Boyo', and that one day the chickens will come home to roost.

The point of this is that in spite of the deluge of affection, which you inspired, I find myself thinking of the three miserable sods who stayed away from the funeral. Years ago, I lent one of these £5,000, and he repaid us, not in cash but in the currency of calumny.

Quite deliberately, he and I now go to different pubs, and of late he has been telling his cronies that the loan was not a loan at all. Now he alleges that it was a wedding present from me to him, and that I asked for its return out of pique and pettiness.

With your passion for justice, you had more sense of honour than anyone I ever knew, I think you would like me to inform his cronies – although they must already know – that the fellow is, in this instance certainly, an arrant liar.

Friday

I sold your car today, didn't haggle, just wanted it gone. The nice man who bought it was virtually my only human contact, apart from people stopping me on the street. What a miserable creature a spoiled husband is! When he is at last alone, he does not know how to look after himself, and if he does know, he doesn't care to. The scales are shifting, though: I am beginning to feel as sorry for myself as for you.

Saturday

Panache, our Balinese, is a glutton, and seems set on turning our apartment into a Child's Garden of Sick. He makes it a point of honour always to throw up twice; which means that when you find one *petit cadeau*, you must search for its twin. Gladys, our tortoiseshell, known as Strumpet Kitty, is beginning to fret. She all but weeps when I stroke her. As for The Pooka, an old friend of yours came a-visiting today, and when she got home she found him, a stowaway, in the rear seat of her car. I have heard of bereaved cats leaving home, but this is absurd.

Sunday

'Know thyself' is one of the maxims inscribed on the Temple of Apollo at Delphi, and savage experience has taught me what disasters await if I as much as touch a frying pan. Which is why this morning, realising that I had forgotten what a fried egg tasted like, I ventured into the newish *Idlewilde*, on St Patrick's Road, or the Bus Lane, as we natives call it. I still cannot say if this is a coffee shop, a *café*, a *konditorei*, or a *trattoria*, as I was not in it long enough to find out.

A dark young lady, who was not a native of these climes, hovered with her order pad, and I told her that, if she pleased, I would like some breakfast. She stared and said 'Breakadafasta?' in her native Nowhere-ese.

'Yes, please, breakadafasta,' I said with linguistic aplomb.

She consulted the chap behind the counter, whom I think I last saw cutting Humphrey Bogart's head off in *The Treasure of the Sierra Madre*. She came back and said 'Breakadafasta stoppa at twelve o'clocka.'

Triumphantly, I told her that the time was still five minutes before twelve o'clocka. I showed her my watch.

I even showed her the Rolex I keep in my trousers' pocket (it's a long story). She was unmoved and gave-a-da-shrugga. I went home and made a sandwich, all the while wondering whether the management kept continental time or if the non-existence of breakadafasta perhaps accounted for the 'Idle' in *Idlewilde*.

Later, watching *The Last of the Summer Wine* I reflected that the writer was making an endless feast of Compos death. The revelation that on Thursdays he secretly visited a gorgeously leggy blonde (Liz Fraser) was pushing it a bit, even if he and she had ferrets in common. You, though, would have laughed a lot and wept a little, and I found myself wanting to tape it for you. No more sharing, aye, there's the rub.

Afterwards, I went to *La Strada* for dinner and tried to reread Maugham's great story, 'The Outstation'. The staff, as always, are kindness itself, but the shrieking of infants was merciless. I was in sympathy with Anthony Hope, he of *The Prisoner of Zenda*, who on the first night of *Peter Pan* was heard to intone: 'Oh, for an hour of Herod!'

As of midnight, April is over, and thank God for that.

Love,
Jack

4

Dear Paule,

No offence, and bless all those who wrote or who spoke and still speak to me in the town, but I am drowning in sympathy. Last evening at the National Concert Hall people kept telling me how brave I was to be there, and an exquisitely tactful lady said: 'It must be terrible having to go back to an empty house.' I fled from her.

I could have told her that the house is not empty; it has three loving and loved, if somewhat bewildered, mogs in it. What is more, and to use an awesomely nail-on-the-head expression offered to me by a Church of Ireland clergyman, it is 'haunted by absence'.

The reason I was so 'brave' – which is perhaps a synonym for crassly indiscreet – as to turn up at the NCH is that this was Veronica McSwiney's birthday concert, and Ronnie and you were friends. And it was lovely to meet the stupendous Suzanne Murphy and renew acquaintance with Richard Baker, a lovely man. Eileen Pearson, another friend of yours and mine, had allowed me to escort her.

The day after you died so suddenly, our splendid and forthright family doctor telephoned me in what approximated to shock. She said, calling a spade a bloody shovel: 'If it was you now, I could have understood it.' This seasoned my grief with a sense of guilt, I felt as if I had let her down; and so it was almost furtively that I arrived in Paris today.

There are two islands in the Seine. The Ile de la Cité is the glamorous one where the tourists pour out of their coaches from Leipzig or Madrid and stand in line waiting to climb the towers of Notre Dame; but just yards away are the narrow streets of the Ile Saint Louis, where one might be in a small provincial town. I am staying at the Hotel du Jeu de Paume. This is on the site of a seventh century 'palm' game, the forerunner of tennis. My room is poky, I tell the patronne that it is '*sombre*', and she replies, irrefutably, 'but, monsieur, the sun is not shining!'

In the evening, I meet my friend of 40 years, Mark Grantham, and we have a wonderful dinner at *Le Vieux Bistro*, where the *boeuf bourguignon* is as light as a soufflé. We talk about love. Grantham was widowed five years ago. He is made of sterner stuff than I, and in his vocabulary, the word 'love' is reserved for his late wife, Mary, and her alone. As for me, there are dear friends of whom I use the term and who use it to me. However, I am not in love with any of them – you alone must endure that burden. Am I indulging in semantics? I hope not.

After dinner, we walk all the way to the Place de la

Bastille and back to the flood-lit Notre Dame. I am pooped by then and not a little drunk; the hotel concierge smirks as I take my room key.

Friday

Am paying a fair price for last evening's indulgence. Grantham appears at midday, having had his usual brisk 90-minute forced march around the Luxembourg Garden. We have a salad for lunch and catch a bus to Pigalle, where, as a dawny youth, I stayed in the *Grand Hotel Laval*, which was not in the least grand.

I recall my very first breakfast in Paris, which I took at a bar counter, assuming that because of this there would be no waiter to tip. To my mortification, I was chased down the street by an old harridan of a patronne, screeching '*Service, monsieur, service!*'

Grantham, although American-born, is an Irish citizen and intends moving back to Dublin. I, on the other hand, have no idea of what the future holds; now that you have so unkindly left me, I shall have to give the torment of living alone a fair try until I cease, if I ever do, to be 'haunted by absence'. Quite rationally, I do think that dying might be easier. When I mentioned this to Danielle, she emailed back to say that losing one parent might be deemed a misfortune; whereas to lose two of them would be 'Bracknelly'.

Saturday

I detest mobile phones as nasty, intrusive, yuppy toys, and this morning while crossing Boulevard Saint Germain I all but jump out of my skin as my own goes off. I keep it for my personal use in emergencies, and this is the first time in two years that the thing has ever emitted a beep. Only two people have my number; and one of them – today's caller – is Danielle in London.

She asks after me. I tell her that Paris was not a good idea; I am a walking misery-guts. As for her, she says that mornings are not her happiest time. Her misery on top of mine is, as weights go, on the heavy side.

The weather is beautiful and so are the Parisiennes. Shakespeare wrote that it is the bright day that brings forth the adder; but in Paris what sunshine brings forth are feminine bosoms – the Place Saint Germain resembles hangars filled with Zeppelins. Grantham and I sit on the terrace of *Les Deux Magots*, and I think of that old fraud, Ernest Hemingway, whose local this was before he started killing animals to prove he was butch. Give me Scott Fitzgerald and *Gatsby* any day.

We go to *Brentano's* for a browse, and on the way back to the Ile Saint Louis the skies open. There are cries of *'Zut, alors!'* and *'Incroyable!'* It makes the afternoon downpour in Singapore seem like a drizzle. We sit in a café, bone-dry in the middle of Niagara, and at last the rain stops and the city shakes itself like a dog after a swim.

Later, we meet for dinner at *Le Trumilou*, a bistro where we were once four instead of, at present, a miserable two. A piano-accordionist plays touristy tunes – 'Sous les Ponts de Paris' and the like. I ask him if he knows one of your favourites, 'La Valse Brune' and he does. It is not one of my better ideas.

Sunday

Sunshine, bells, crowds, skateboarders, the roars of motorcycles and the laughter of Japs. We walk to the Left Bank, past *Shakespeare and Co.*, up under the Boulevard Saint Michel and sit under the trees in the Luxembourg Garden. There is a stunning exhibition of aerial photographs: 'La Terre Vue du Ciel'. The colours are so dazzling as to seem surreal.

In the evening a gorgeous (female) taxi driver takes me to the *Polidor Restaurant* in the Rue Monsieur le Prince. Cleverly, she displays a photo of Harvey Keitel which conceals the tariff on her meter. The *Polidor* – a haunt of Joyce and the 1930s gang – seems frozen in time with its oil-cloth and paper coverings on the tables. It takes no reservations and accepts no cards. It is cheap, the food is excellent and the waitresses are the kind one takes home to mother. Go early; it is popular. Also, one shares a table with other diners, and we fall into talk with Larry, a New York psychiatrist, and his wife Judy, who takes a platonic shine to me.

It is one of the universal truths that all psychiatrists

are as barmy as a Hallowe'en brack. No one has ever worked out which came first, as it were: the chicken or the egg. I mean, one wonders whether a shrink contracts nuttiness from his patients, or whether he has gone in for his particular line of work because he was a fruitcake to begin with.

At any rate, Larry is crazier than both Frasier and Niles put together. When he and Judy leave the restaurant, he dumps her, walking off in a jealous snit. We find this out because, as we sit outside a Left Bank café after dinner listening to an Australian lady telling us a dirty joke about a parrot, Judy comes upon us. (Paris is a very small city.) Like Chaucer's 'verray, parfait, gentil knyght', we escort her to her hotel, where Larry awaits. Even as I write, she is probably floating in several pieces down the Seine.

Monday

This evening we are to take a posh boat trip, dinner included, and I need to buy a shirt. Naturally, I head for *Charvet* on the Rue de Rivoli. But it is closed, for today is the fifty-fifth anniversary of VE Day, with a great parade on the Champs-Élysées. A sign in the window says, 'By appointment to Mr Charles Haughey, C. H.' A Frenchman comes and stands beside me. He wonders aloud if the 'C. H.' stands for 'Companion of Honour'. I tell him no, that it is purely an Irish distinction, an abbreviation for 'cute hoor'.

(Come to think of it, Mr Haughey's own initials are C. H. Why did we not take the hint?)

The feet, to use a phrase of yours, are walked off of me. Indeed, as I tramp this way and that and the day gets hotter, I can hear your voice saying 'How much further?' and 'I'm not able for this'. If I look at a backless, frontless dress in the window of a haute couture establishment, I hear you laugh in disbelief and say, 'How would you like me in that?' So, to shut you up, I take you to the pictures.

Actually, you would have liked *Hypnose*, which is worth watching out for, although I have no idea what the American title may be. A young New York workman (Kevin Bacon) submits himself to hypnotism and is such a 'natural' that a door to the occult opens in his mind. He is haunted by the ghost of a girl who several months ago disappeared from home, and when he goes into another trance and receives the one-word message 'Dig!' we know that women in the audience are likely to have a bad hair day.

Tuesday

For my last evening in Paris, Grantham takes me to the *Polidor* again. There is no sign of Larry and Judy, and I am not surprised. She is probably bobbing past Le Havre by now.

Wednesday

And so home, and there are another hundred or so letters waiting. Some of them are simple messages of condolence; others are from people who themselves are bereaved; and of course there are those who tell me that my wife is not dead but merely 'gone before'. Well, without an atom of disrespect to you and, on the contrary, in all love, I would say that given the way you drove, it would be in character.

Love,
Jack

5

Friday

Dear Paule,

If you will pardon an acute Irishism, life without you is no better than it was, but at least it is becoming less worse. And you will be surprised to know that you are still alive. It is four weeks now, but because of a backlog in a toxicology department, a death certificate cannot be issued. Small wonder, then, that last night I dreamt I heard voices and saw you and Danielle coming in out of a pool of darkness at our front door and laughing. It was a rough awakening.

Already I have learnt what, in a realistic sense, is the essence of living alone. It is when one drops a sock on the floor, it will not within an hour or so vanish magically into a drawer or a washing machine. It will stay lying there until either hell freezes over or the person who dropped it picks it up.

This morning, Danielle, bless her, arrived for the weekend, and it took me 95 minutes to drive the sixteen miles to the airport; which amounts to an average speed of ten miles per hour. We boast that we have Europe's fastest-growing economy, and yet our roads are of the third world. Ours must be the only western

European capital without a rail link to its airport.
Where, one asks, is the money that would pay for it?
Embezzled, probably; that's where.

Really, the arch-villain, C. J. Haughey should have
been given a stiff brandy and then left alone in a room
with a loaded shillelagh. Nah, he would only have
flogged it to a tourist, swearing that it was Brian Boru's
dildo.

Today, cooling my wheels, behind a revolving
cement mixer on the East Wall Road and anticipating
the delights of the pot-holes on the Richmond and Grace
Park roads just ahead, I have time to read the name-
plate on the door of a terrace house. It says: *Shambles*.
Well, at least someone is telling it like it is.

After four weeks, the mail has slackened off, praise
be. Item: a postcard comes, delivered from New York
by courier, and it is from Gabriel Byrne, whom I hardly know and you met only once and fleetingly. Many
years ago, I mentioned in this column that I had been
searching for Somerset Maugham's anthology, *Tellers of
Tales*, and this Byrne of Byrnes, whom I had never even
met, sent it to me. A good and kindly man.

Item: a theatre director says that out of respect for
my bereavement, he will not pester me to come to too
many rehearsals of a play of mine that is to be revived.
It is strange that people push solitude at one, when
being alone is what one most dreads.

Item: As if what has happened is not enough, I

open a letter addressed to you from the husband of your oldest friend Sigrid, who lives in Philadelphia and has not been well. He says you will be sorry to learn that his wife 'passed away' three weeks ago. Of course, it may be that you know that already and the pair of you are already colloguing and puffing away on the cigarettes that helped kill both of you.

And, item: Our hoaxer friend is still at it. Now he has forged a subscription for me to the *New Yorker* among other magazines. Or, rather, a copy has arrived at this address, giving the addressee's name – mine, that is – as 'Mr R. Sole' (just try saying it out loud, my dear). You and I know who the Dalkey culprit may be and what this is all about. It is because, unforgivably, we once did him and his lady wife several favours, such as taking them on holiday. Good deeds never go unpunished.

Saturday
It is good to have Dan home if only for a weekend. She has been putting part of your life, your clothes that is, into black plastic bags which are to go to *Centrecare*. Like the true and thrifty Belgian you were, you threw nothing away. And, while my own weakness has always been for hoarding books, yours was for shoes. 'My God,' Dan said to me today, 'Mum's real name was Imelda Marcos!'

As often as not, you would sail past a footwear

shop with a disdainful sniff and a verdict of 'Rubbish!' but one day, in the canal town of Redon, you were torn between two pairs of shoes, just in from Paris, and both equally to be lusted after. 'What'll I do?' you moaned.

'Buy them both!' I said, brutally cutting the Gordian knot.

In the end, you did buy both, and your idea of taking the curse off your extravagance was to make me your partner in crime; i.e., you bought *me* a pair, too. They were Church's shoes, the best in the world, and I still wear them.

This evening, with our friend Max, we had an excellent dinner at *The Vico*, in Dalkey. Or it would have been excellent, but you sat there and glared at me, as usual, for eating too much bread and not enough vegetables. Earlier this week in Paris, you were with me so constantly that at one point I all but urged you not to cross a street against the lights. My fancy took over, and I thought of the graveyard scene in the play, *Our Town*, in which the dead are still with us for a time, waiting to be weaned away from the earth.

I even sat in a café and worked out the plot of a story I shall probably never write. In this, a bereaved man, walking around a strange city, believes himself to be accompanied by his wife's spirit. The thought occurs to him that perhaps she inhabits a half-world in which she does not yet know she is dead. She continues to be with him in cafés, buses, streets and churches. At last in his wanderings, he espies an old friend of the family, but to his astonishment it is the phantom wife who goes up to this person and speaks to him.

She says: 'My late husband is following me wherever I go. He doesn't yet know that he is dead.'

You always liked stories that had a twist in the tail.

And did I tell you a truth spoken by our friend, Mark, who himself has been a widower these five years?

'All one really wants,' he said, 'is a hug now and again.'

If I may adapt this into the patois of P. G. Wodehouse, one would like to enjoy the occasional ham sandwich, without the feeling that one was making a down payment on the Empress of Blandings. (The Empress, of course, was a champion porker.)

Sunday

This morning on the Andy O'Mahony radio show there was much eulogising about the Irish entry in last evening's Eurovision song contest. This annual explosion of atonal infantilism has now descended to a nadir of witless self-parody, so that Terry Wogan's mockery is merely coals to Newcastle or, in this instance, bacon to Denmark.

Mr O'Mahony cutely sang dumb, while a lady and may God forgive her! gushed like Old Faithful, buttering up the perpetrator of the Irish entry, who almost levitated above Montrose on a cloud of ecstatic self-delusion. It was probably the worst song I have ever heard in a long lifetime of suffering. To say that it was rubbish would be to insult our dustbin. It was moronic, mawkish, maudlin, trite and tuneless. Honestly, Paule; it was enough to make you turn in your urn.

You know that rosewood desk which was your private domain? Well, this evening I opened it and binned all the wallets of holiday photographs, from as far away as Young Island and Bequia on the edge of the Grenadines and, to the east, China, Thailand and the River Kwai, bridge and all. We rode quarter-horses on the slopes of Old Baldy above the Pecos River in New Mexico, flew over Alaskan glaciers in float-planes and looked for, and found, sea-otters off the Isle of Eriska, north of Oban.

We had the best dinner of our lives at *Les Frères Troisgros* in Roanne, where you over-balanced and fell off your sofa-seat. Two waiters picked you up, while another ran to replace your spilled aperitif, all within seconds. We climbed a no-longer-dormant volcano, Soufriere on St Vincent, detested the manicured stuffiness of Barbados, drank a lethal cocktail called Between the Sheets at midnight in Funchal Bay, and the even deadlier Moose's Milk, off Acapulco.

There were cruises to the Odessa Steps, to Istanbul, to Iceland, where we rode Skidoos across a glacier, to Nagasaki, where a Japanese gentleman and I bowed and embraced to the tune of *One Fine Day*, and a trip by Orient Express from which you assisted me to throw a pair of trousers at dead of night in darkest Bulgaria. In Capri, you saw a dress that was half the price you had paid for it in Dublin, so of course you bought it all over again. And there were snapshots from a dozen French canals.

This evening, I threw them all away without opening the wallets, but there was one black-and-white photograph that slipped into open view. It was taken in the Abbey Theatre bar, and in it, Fergus Bourke, squatting on his hunkers, was convulsed with laughter. You and I were sitting on one of the low padded stools (you had smashing legs), and I wore the smug raconteur's smile of one who has just delivered a zinger. As for you, you were an adoring audience, you never let on that it was the twentieth time you had heard a story.

I refuse to believe that all the good and bad moments of one's life simply disappear. The jokes and laughter, the books read and films seen, the work done and the roads walked; the good company and the grass lain in; the friendships, broken as well as made, and the songs sung – I believe they still exist, and we have not the foggiest notion of what Time is.

Perhaps J. B. Priestley's theory is true. When we journey from, say, Illyria to Fiddler's Green, Illyria does not cease to exist because it is behind us and out of sight. And if one is reading a book, the early pages don't simply vanish; they are still there as we move on towards the final chapter. I believe that that is true of living, and that life, with all that is in it, continues to exist, between covers. The universe wastes nothing.

Monday

I drive Danielle to the airport, and this time at least there are no tears, apart from tears of fury because on this occasion it took nearly two hours. She is to return for another visit the week after next, for the twenty-eight will be our forty-fifth anniversary, and I cannot go it alone. If it is tears you want, hang on until then; I can promise you buckets.

Love,
Jack

6

Dear Paule,

Stephen Durbridge and Wendy Gresser flew over from London this morning to give me lunch at *L'Ecrivain*. I had wondered what could be of such moment as to bring not just one, but both my agents to Dublin. Was I being drummed out of The Agency for conduct unbecoming? Or perhaps I had been selected to write *Titanic 2, The Iceberg's Story?*

It transpired that the pair had come all this way for no other reason than to utter whatever the English equivalent is of 'Sorry for your trouble'. As the saying goes, I am the kind who cries at card tricks, and, when confronted with sheer goodness for its own sake, I dissolved. So there I was making a show of myself in the best restaurant in town – and all on your account.

They wanted to talk about my novel, *A Wild People*, which of course they have read in typescript. Stephen begged to be told which character was a portrait of what person in real life. Naturally, I recoiled from the suggestion that I would ever dream of clothing actual people in the raiment of fiction. Perish the very thought. Tut, in fact, and tush as well.

We talked about your funeral, over four weeks ago, and they were incredulous that a certain theatrical Pooh-Bah, whose youngest is my godson, did not attend or send a card. I suggested to my agents that they had a poor knowledge of human nature, and that the fellow's quaint idea of integrity is to give up a friend for Lent.

When they had departed for their six o'clock flight home, I gave myself a good talking-to and came to what is an important decision, always assuming that I can stand firm. It is this, but bear with me a moment.

There are two kinds of grief. The first is for the person who is no more, and it has to do with loss. It is about a life cut short; hopes blighted and good times taken away. It echoes the grief of those left behind who, to use a word that is constantly flung at me these days, are 'devastated'. It is about aloneness, the amputation of a limb and the delusion that it is still there. And, in my own case, the suddenness of what happened has put pictures into my mind's eye that I would rather not see.

I expect that I will drown in this kind of grief for always. The other kind is more self-pitying and, perhaps, self-dramatising. It says 'Oh, God, what's going to happen to *me*?' It sees a wasteland of purposeless days to come; it is about the impossibility of survival. Death becomes the tragedy of the bereaved, not of the departed. For five weeks, I have had a wallow in this as well as the other, more selfless, kind.

Well, today, with my agent's visit, I encountered a kind of goodness that Pooh-Bah, bless him, may never begin to know or understand. This evening, I remembered that I am enriched with an incredible daughter in whom you still live, many good friends, three mogs, loving and loved, a view of the sea, work to do and a world to live in. The time of feeling sorry for myself is over, as of now, and no longer am I, like Mrs Gummidge, 'a lone, lorn creetur with whom everything goes contrairy'. Feeling sorry for *you*, Paule, is, of course, quite another matter.

Thursday

As I am making short work of lunch in our local pub, an elderly lady comes up. She does not condole, instead, she says, straight off: 'You never said hello to me on the street, but your wife always did.' Translated, into Dalkeyspeak, this means: 'Your wife was a lovely person, but you are a surly sod.' Mind, the old faggot may be right. You had a smile for every dog and devil on the street; then you came home and, with an end-of-the-world gasp of cod incredulity, said: 'You never left the lavatory seat up again?'

Meanwhile, a Derry publisher wants me to contribute to a book all about Ireland. It is to show outsiders a 'positive' and 'affirmative' landscape. In short, it will be the usual pack of dewy-eyed porkies.

My Ireland is a country of incredible beauty, ravaged by 'developers'. It is a haven for the very rich and a purgatory for the poor although all praise to Tony O'Reilly for at least using his wealth to bring a Monet painting into the country. The corruption that is being exposed each day would make a South American dictator writhe in envy, and yet there is more than the suspicion that all this is only the iceberg's tip.

Values are non-existent. A few weeks ago, RTE showed a programme in which Terry Keane, looking more and more like a down-market Brenda Blethyn, portrayed herself as a kind of heroic all-for-love royal mistress rather than as a grubby chancer's bit on the side. (One marvels that they could do no better than each other!) No offence to her, but is this the zenith of what we can achieve in the line of scarlet women? Pinkish, rather, and with the colour running in the wash.

And, the other day, a tiny thing, but a microcosm: there were no English newspapers because, I was told, a machine at Easons had broken down. A few days later, there was a contretemps at the airport and the cross-channel papers could not be unloaded. Next week we shall doubtless hear that one of the sled-dogs has been taken sick. And wherever one drives there are roadworks, and yet the roads never get any better.

More? Last week, a proven rogue, bribe-taker and blackguard was given a punishment of fourteen days suspension by his party. In short, getting caught is the only real crime in the eyes of the Fianna Fáil Mafia.

And it was ever thus. Back in the golden days of Seán Lemass, who is much revered as the architect of the New Ireland, I knew a Flemish businessman named Warnant: a fat, bluff charmer, who had a plump finger in every pie. He told me the secret of his success. Whenever he needed a special favour, a door to be opened, or a queue to be jumped, he simply arranged to play poker with the Taoiseach, Lemass, and took care to lose, heavily. Money lost at cards was tribunal-proof.

No. I told the Derry publisher that he would not care to print what I would write.

Friday

Lunch at *Brownes* with a close friend. We talked about you, of course, and, apropos of something that was said, I remembered our very first date, nearly fifty years ago. I was producing a Christmas programme of plays at my old school, Presentation College in Glasthule, and I asked you to come and help with the make-up. After the show, the Brothers invited us into the parlour, and bottles of Guinness were produced.

A friend of mine, Jimmy Keogh – who is still a friend of mine – had appeared with me that evening in the Lady Gregory one-acter, *The Workhouse Ward*. Jimmy was learning to play the clarinet, and kept his instrument, unscrewed into three sections, in a small leather case. When he had gone home, the Superior, Brother Fergal, threw out the question across the table: 'What is it that Jimmy has in that black case?'

To which you, the Belgian who knew nothing of Irish vernacular, replied, brightly and innocently: 'His flute!'

Brother Fergal spilled his stout, and I knew then that I would marry you. There was honestly no other possibility.

Saturday

A reader, well-meaning, no doubt, has suggested that there may be those who will dispute my right and question my motives in writing you these open letters. Well, I have a 'right' to do whatever I like, always provided as Mrs Pat said regarding sex, I don't do it in the street and frighten the horses. As regard motives, however, I am on shakier ground.

And yet at today's Church of Ireland bazaar which was not, as I had feared, a fête worse than death three ladies came up separately and thanked me for sharing my thoughts and, in one case, helping her to cope with a personal bereavement. This was not my purpose; rather the idea was the selfish one of helping me with mine. No matter, in fact, all to the good, and just for a few more weeks I would like to keep writing to you.

Mind, in the letters I still receive, we are being mythologised, you and I, as an ideal couple, a kind of devoted Darby and Joan; whereas up to three years ago at any rate we fought like Kilkenny cats. What all this is about is not happiness, but loving. There is a hell of a difference.

Sunday

You were forever acquiring cuts, scratches, scalds and burns. Well, today there are assorted bright splats of blood all over the kitchen floor. I wonder from which orifice I am haemorrhaging, then I realise that I have sliced open the knuckle of my little finger with the lid of a tin of Whiskas.

I hold my hand under a cold tap, and the water pressure opens the flap of the wound still further. A half-hour creeps by, and the bleeding will not stop. I make a dog's dinner of trying to peel open a piece of sticking plaster with my left hand. Meanwhile, Gladys is in seventh heaven playing with the spilled contents of a box of band-aids.

From outside the hall door, I can espy our downstairs neighbour exchanging the time of day with The Pooka while unaware that something other than raindrops is falling on her head. Kindly woman that she is, she comes up and binds the injured pinky until it is tighter than a bricklayer on a Saturday night. You would have done no less, but first you would have looked at the bleeding finger and said: 'So what will you do for an encore?'

It was not altogether a bloody day. Father Murnaghan and the Reverend Ben Neil of St Patrick's led an ecumenical pilgrimage to Dalkey Island. It was lovely, with hymns and a few prayers. There was sunshine, with soaring clouds, an infinity of blue sky and the sensation of being afloat on a great green ship. For the first time since the funeral, and without romancing, I had the sensation that you were all about.

The woeful news is that Father Martin Murnaghan, having brought Christianity to Dalkey, is about to leave us for a parish of his own near Castleknock. If they had to upgrade him, could it not have been to the Vatican? – this was not merely a blunder, but a cardinal error. For me, and without being disrespectful, it was like finding the perfect poker-player, and then discovering that he has converted to bridge.

Monday
A scrawl of a note, with an illegible signature and no return address. The message is simple: 'Dear Jack. Follow Paule. Ha-ha.' It seems, my dear, that we are back to business as usual.

Love,
Jack

7

Dear Paule,

If smiling is permitted wherever you are, you might enjoy a news item, which was in yesterday's *Irish Times* under the caption: 'Two arrested for tyre-slashing'. It read: 'Ennis gardaí said yesterday they have arrested two local teenagers in connection with the slashing of tyres of 28 cars in a car park in Ennis at the weekend. A sharp instrument was recovered, and a file is being sent to the DPP.'

I e-mailed this to Danielle in London and this morning received the following: 'That should nail them, unless someone throws a spanner in the works. If they get a prison sentence, how will they get on with the screws?' Well, that, I'm afraid, my dear, is the sort of daughter you reared.

How am I getting on? Well, last Monday, and thank you for asking, was the worst day since the main event. Without any discernible 'trigger', it was ten hours of walk-into-the-sea depression: a dose of the glums like you would not believe, with nothing to do but sit and out-weep Niobe and play solitaire. There are those who tell me – and they do, *they do!* – that grief must be given full bay-at-the-moon howls, otherwise one is building up a huge coop of chickens that will inevitably come home to roost. On the other hand, one might consider that no friends, no matter how devoted, want a lachrymose skeleton at their feast and a blanket that is forever wringing wet.

On Tuesday, I was to meet Emer O'K at *Les Frères Jacques*, but lunch went for its tea when I had difficulty in waking dozy Gladys from her night's sleep. And no, dear, I have not taken another woman to bed; Gladys continues to be our tortoiseshell. So I conveyed her to Pete Wedderburn, who continues to be our vet. He diagnosed a mild infection and gave her an injection, and *that* bloody well woke her up.

In the afternoon I buried my pride and inflicted myself on our long-suffering friends, Bernard and Gloria, in Greystones. 'Just a bite in the kitchen,' Bernard said to allay my craw-thumping guilt, and then Gloria, the hussy, went and served up a delicious three-course dinner with wine.

Which brings me to yesterday, Wednesday, when I met Gillian Bowler for lunch at *L'Ecrivain*, and as usual she was the most commonsensical person in the wide world. We talked of cabbages and kings and, of course, you. At one point, I told her, such was my confusion of mind: 'I don't know whether the bloody woman loved me or not.' At this, having sown the wind, I promptly reaped the whirlwind (*Hosea*, 8; vii).

'Oh, come off it!' Gillian, the most excellent of her sex, said, with the nearest to a snort she could manage. 'A woman doesn't all the time go around mouthing "I love you". What she does is, she cooks something you like, even if it's not good for you; she irons a shirt and does not see it as a chore; she cleans your workroom when it doesn't need it; she sits through a play she hates – such as Shakespeare in your case – and she bores her friends with "Jack says this" or "Jack says that". That's what loving is!'

Well, I think that is a fair summary of it; and, with which she changed the subject. Collapse, as they say, of stout party.

Which brings us to today, and there was an e-mail from our friend, Joe Contino, in Chicago, who returned from a long cruise only a week ago and was shattered on hearing my news. He wants to come and visit me and be a comfort. At first I said yes, then I begged him to stay where he is.

I was thinking of our first meeting five years ago on board the *Royal Viking Sun*, crossing the Atlantic to New York. Joe had been recently widowed (everywhere I look these days I see bloody widowers!): a tall grey-haired figure in his early-to-mid-60s. He had a gap between his front teeth and walked with feet splayed out, like a haemorrhoidal duck. Well, on the last night of the cruise, I was sitting alone in the gloom of the Look-out Bar when he came up and kissed me on the cheek.

I stared at him in absolute, dumbstruck horror; then looked around for you, hoping you would appear and save me from this depraved lunatic. Then Joe said: 'Well, I can't help it. You're my friend, and I'm Italian, and I'm sentimental!'

Well, I'm Irish, and I'm sentimental, too, and I have a vision of Joe coming here, and both of us drinking too much J&B far into the night and getting maudlin. (And if he became sentimental again, I might burst him.) So I begged him to hold off for a month or so – at least until I read the first chapter of Delia Smith's cookery book and can change the cat litter without the apartment looking like Brittas Bay after a bank holiday.

Meanwhile, the daily post-bag has shrunk to its usual trickle of spring water laced with the occasional dash of paraquat. For example, a certain doctor of Oranmore writes in surprise that I have repeated 'that tiresome and incorrect canard' (was there ever a canard that was correct?): i.e., that ours must be the only Western European capital without a rail-link to its airport. He refutes this by naming Oslo and Reykjavik, and gamely admits that there is no railway in Iceland, which just possibly could be the reason.

Actually, it wasn't a canard – Paddy-bashing, that is – just carelessness on my part. But surely, the point is that neither Oslo nor Reykjavik *needs* a rail-link, because the road traffic is not nearly heavy enough to justify it. Dublin has gone out of control and is well on its way towards wholesale gridlock.

The roads, narrow, broken and often pot-holed, are a joke that turns sour when one considers what one must pay to drive on them (surely it cannot *all* have been pocketed by Charlie Haughey?). When the DART service came about, there was an opportunity to create a spur-line to the airport, but the moment was lost.

The education of an Irish driver stops short at pointing the car, (mis)using the pedals and going through red lights. The business of signalling, lane discipline and parking are unlearnt arts. In my own town, cars speed through Castle Street so blindly that a bereaved man could commit suicide without even trying. And there is no uniformed figure in view to stop them.

Having dismounted from this hobbyhorse, I walked to my local pub where, at the end of my working day, and if I am without a dinner engagement, I treat myself to two drinks. And here, I learned another lesson of alone-ness. As I was about to leave, a friend came in and urged me to stay and join him in a drink. I told him no; I had to get home.

I was walking towards the door when it occurred to me that I did not have to get home, because there was no one there. Whatever they may say, freedom is overrated.

Saturday

In Belgium, there are usually two weddings: a civil ceremony performed at the *mairie* or town hall, followed by a church wedding which usually happens the following day. Forty-five years ago today, the mayor of Chaudfontaine, your native village five miles from Liege, tied the knot. We then had cold cuts for lunch, and off we went to the pictures to see *The Woman Who Invented Love*, starring a splendidly pneumatic Italian actress named Sylvana Pampanini.

We were not yet married in the sight of God, or so your family believed, or at least pretended to. You and your Dublin-based parents were staying in the home of your uncle and aunt on the Avenue William Grisard and I was lodged in the attic bedroom. That night, sentries were posted on the stairs in case I sneaked down one floor (or you sneaked up one) to consummate the nuptials.

Probably today, matters are ordered differently. No doubt there are bits of cardboard pinned all the way up the stairs, each one with a crayoned finger pointing the way in case the bridegroom might get lost and end up with Aunt Nelly or, worse, Uncle Gaston. There may even be a discreet paper trail of confetti.

Next day, there was the church wedding, to which we were driven in an open car, you radiant in a champagne-coloured dress and I burning with acute embarrassment. After the ceremony, as we walked from the altar, children came up and presented you with flowers in vases. Starting as you meant to continue, you thrust them at me, and I dumped them in the holy water font. Down the years I can still hear the clatter and crash.

At the wedding, there was a cake of ice-cream, surmounted by two vanilla doves, one for each of us: *les colombes de bonheur*. The party afterwards was spread through three rooms. One was for the more sedate guests, and another was peopled with hirsute old harridans who cackled at filthy stories, told in Walloon, and urged me to come and sit on their laps. In the third room your uncle Gaston, who was a stockbroker of simian aspect, denuded himself to the waist – it was his party piece – and displayed more hair on his back than most orang-utans have on their fronts.

For the honeymoon, we went on a coach trip from Brussels to Brunate on Lake Como, then back to Paris. Our fellow-passengers might have been characters in a third-rate British film comedy. We gave them nicknames. There was a cheese-pilfering lady named Fanny by Gaslight, and a prophet of doom known as Cheerful Charlie. There was a Hyacinth Bucket clone we dubbed Mrs Who-Flung, who, on learning of a rail strike in Britain, said: 'How tragic that one can't be with the Old Country at a time like this!'

There were a bookie and his wife: a lady with size ten feet who wore size four sandals, a bullet-headed groper known as Mussolini, and a dear old lady, a vicar's daughter, who was the spitting image of Margaret Rutherford. I picked mountain flowers for her, and her painting of them is still in our bedroom.

And there was John Huxley, who went on a second holiday every year after betting on the winner of the Derby, a tip from a top trainer, first name Scobie. Because of him I emptied our small bank account and, without telling you, put it all on St Paddy, which romped home at 12 to 1. So, as honeymoons go, ours was pretty good.

Love,
Jack

8

Sunday

Dear Paule,

Do you recall an evening in London back in 1969 when we had as our houseguest an actor friend, whom I will call Cousin Enda? The three of us were watching an excerpt on television from a new Japanese film called *Double Suicide*. The scene featured a man and a woman dressed in kimonos and kneeling face to face in front of a screen on which there was Japanese writing. True to the title, they proceeded to disembowel themselves.

There were about five minutes of grunting, gasping, terminal gurgling and other manifestations of Oriental discomfort. Like Charles II, the pair took an unconscionable time a-dying, and we looked on in silent fascination. At last, they expired, whereupon Cousin Enda, who is the wittiest man I know, present company excepted, spoke up.

He said: 'Of course you know what's written on that screen?' he said. 'It says: Joe Lynch is coming to tea.' Your hoots of laughter kept me awake until the small hours.

I recall an evening you and I spent with Joe when he regaled us with a dozen or so anecdotes, all hugely entertaining. Then you tottered off to bed, exhausted perhaps, whereupon our guest said to me: 'Now I'll give you the unexpurgated version', and he proceeded to tell the stories over again in the *same order*.

Joe, to put it kindly, would talk a hole in an iron-monger's shop. As was once said of Debbie Reynolds, if you opened the fridge door, he would do twenty minutes. Grangegorman is thronged with play direc-tors with whom he has argued about whether he should cross his legs at the knees in Act One or wait until Act Two and cross them at the ankles, and today in the *Indo* he has been giving out about the miserliness of RTE which has prompted him to leave *Glenroe*.

In my old-fashioned way, I would hold that a villa in Spain is hardly the ideal place for what is known as the poor mouth. It may be that Joe's 'villa' is no more than a two-roomed adobe hut behind a bull-ring or a maracas factory, but I doubt it. If, as I suspect, it has a swimming pool, a lemon tree and year-round sun-shine, then Joe is as likely to obtain public sympathy as Charlie Haughey would be to succeed in touching Ben Dunne's sister for the loan of a fiver until Friday.

I don't know which arrogant sod it was who first said 'Never apologise, never explain', unless it was Ad-miral Lord Fisher, who, in a letter to the *Times* in 1919, added a third precept: 'Never contradict'. Well, my own advice to Joe is: feel free to apologise, explain and contradict until the *toros* come home, but never, never complain, even if you *don't* own a villa in Spain. It is as bad as answering a critic; it marks you down as that most shunnable of God's creatures: a loser.

And I don't know either why I am rabbiting on about a belly-aching actor. Or rather, I do know, for today, my dear, would have been our forty-fifth wedding anniversary, and I want to avoid thinking about it because I get oh, so angry. I recall a conversation with the late playwright and film writer Robert Bolt. There had been a terrible scandal involving his wife, Sarah Miles, and I asked him how he had managed to get over it. 'I didn't,' he said, simply. 'I went around it.'

I thought at the time that he was very wise, and of course he was nothing of the sort. He was dodging the column, and not long afterwards he had a massive stroke. Well, I am trying to get over you, as it were, and fat chance, but just for today and like Robert Bolt and another fugitive from reality, namely Ibsen's Peer Gynt, I am going around about.

Today, Danielle sorted through still more piles of snapshots, which I binned. I already *know* what you looked like. And this evening the kindest of ladies, one whom you adored, gave us a dinner party. The talk was funny and good, and we came to the edge of the precipice only once and steered away just in time. To mix my metaphors, we avoided the reef, went home and made plans for yet another French canal. And don't fret yourself; you'll be there.

Monday

We go to see *Gladiator*, which is bloody great – I mean that literally. And there is historical truth in it of a kind. The emperor Commodus (ad 161–192) was a nasty piece of work, who was seen off, and not a moment too soon, at the behest of his mistress, one Marcia. Actually, she had him strangled by a gladiator who bore the nickname of Narcissus.

Danielle – ex-classics graduates are such know-alls – points out one glaring unlikelihood. The hero Maximus is an acclaimed general and the surrogate son of the emperor Marcus Aurelius, and so he would have had many friends and allies in Rome, in the senate and among the people. And yet he seems to be virtually unknown there. When he removes his mask after a victory in the arena, there is not a single cry of 'Ah, Jay, looka, it's the hard Max.'

It is splendidly old-fashioned stuff, inasmuch as there is villainy in high places, betrayal, tyranny, revenge, suspense and a bloody and applaudable comeuppance. Many of the crowd scenes are done by computer, and I wish they lasted longer, for the eye cannot take in the stunning detail of the 'aerial' shots of Rome and the Coliseum. The spectacle, with apparently a hundred thousand swarming, milling extras, takes the breath away.

You would have hated this film, I suspect. Suspense was not your bag, as they say. I recall that to-

wards the end of *True Crime*, starring the man you always referred to as East Clintwood, you went and hid
in the kitchen. So at least for once I was not wishing
you were with me. You were not at all like a one-time
friend of ours, now a drama critic known as 'Go see',
who used to smack his lips and say: 'I love voilence!'
(sic)

Tuesday
The trickle of letters is in full spate again, and today's
lot includes one from a clergyman acquaintance of
mine, the sort of chap who, I suspect, could find 'ton-
gues in trees, books in the running brooks and ser-
mons in stones.' He addresses me, I think pityingly, as
'my vaguely agnostic friend'. (The word 'agnostic' was
coined by Professor Thomas Huxley in 1869. It was a
made-up word used to define 'those who disclaimed
atheism and believed in an unknown and unknowable
God.')

I have had many heartfelt letters which say that the
writers are praying for Danielle and me. There are
poems, some of which are upsetting to me, such as
Auden's 'Stop all the clocks', spoken in *Four Weddings
and a Funeral*. And there is the familiar and comforting
piece – a straw to be clutched at, but I don't buy it – that
says 'I have merely slipped away into another room.'

The messages that get furthest up my septum,
however, are those that blithely assure me that prayers

are being offered to God to show you mercy. I mean, what need does a good and honourable woman have of mercy, and what is the alternative? Hell? Actually, my idea of hell would be Heaven without you in it.

A reverend lady warns me in her gentle and kindly way that you, Paule, cannot read these weekly letters of mine and that what you are in need of now is prayers. Well, I would ask my correspondent: What do you think these letters of mine are if they are not prayers? And – no mockery intended – how can a soul think without a brain, give praise without lips, see without eyes, hear without ears or love without a heart? As the king of Siam kept saying: 'Is puzzlement'.

Wednesday
And off Danielle goes once again, back 'home' to London. Ours has never been what is described as a touchy-feely kind of family – a quick, embarrassed peck on the cheek, and that is our lot; nor have we gone in for verbal endearments. Having one shy person in a family is wretchedness enough, but three of them is the pits.

After midnight, however, the phone goes and it is Dan to say that she has arrived safely. And this time I manage to say, 'I miss you'. Some lessons do get finally learned, if belatedly. And what did Dan say in reply? I hear you ask. Sorry, but others are earwigging.

Thursday

In case you are wondering how the flesh-and-blood part of me is getting on, well, I have two newly-acquired books in front of me: – *The Tibetan Book of Living* and Dying and Delia Smith's cookbook, *One is Fun* (like hell it is) and I am not sure as to which is the more scary. My self-prepared dinners are in two courses: the first is served at 6.30 p.m., the second – two Alka-Seltzers – at 3.30 a.m.

You were partial to all kinds of fruit except apples, which is why I only now have discovered Copella Apple Juice. It is simply the juice, without additives, and how pleasant it is when something that is good for you is delicious as well. We seem to live in a world of Brussels sprouts, broccoli and women with moustaches – have you noticed that the hairier the female the more insistent she is on being kissed!

Dan and I have been for dinner at *Duzys* in Glasthule. It is a kind of glossy make-over of *Morels* and reminds one of the plain secretary who takes off her spectacles and shakes her hair loose, whereupon the boss says: 'Why, Miss Murgatroyd, you're beautiful!' John Dunne is still cooking, the food is lighter now, but as excellent as before; Stephane has shaved off his Luciferian beard; and my only crib is that the irreplaceable Sandrine is, to coin a word, irreplaced. And it was packed out, and on a Tuesday as well!

And, surrounded by the Ladies Who Lunch, I enjoyed an upmarket banger at *Munkberrys* in Dalkey. When there is femininity all about, one knows that the food will be both sensible and light, and so this gets a definite A-minus. There is a pleasant house wine (white), and I have only two grumbles: the hardwood chairs would make a fakir long for his bed of nails; and if one more otherwise lovesome waitress chirps 'No problem' at me, I swear I shall marry her and beat her every night.

Friday
The Three Kates – Karen Ardiff, Catherine Walsh and Ingrid Craigie – having laid waste to Silicon Valley in Patrick Mason's production of my play, *Love in the Title*, are now off to take Singapore by storm. And so Patrick invites me to have lunch with him and them at *Cooke's Café*.

Alas, a few days ago I discovered some undeveloped rolls of film, and today they turned out to be photos from our holiday last September on the Canal du Midi, and there you are in the sunshine, smiling out at me against the green-as-a-dream background of a lock which, as Paddy Kavanagh said, is Niagarously pouring. So I am hardly in a fit state for the lovely flood of affection lavished on me by the Kates.

All the same, it was a happy lunch. The three were performing in San José, California, when the bad news came. They dedicated that evening's show to you, and each one of them had the uncanny and vivid feeling that at one point in the play you were on stage in spirit.

Anyway, I express the hope that the play will sing in Singapore, bid them farewell, go home, bite the bullet and put the canal photo of you in a frame Then I stick another snapshot of you above my desk. You will never know the effort that took.

Oh, by the way a fool of a woman sent a card wishing us a happy anniversary. And an elderly bird caught my arm in the supermarket and said 'Are you over the shock yet?' Without waiting for an answer, she added cheerfully: 'No, and you never will be!'

Love,
Jack

9

Dear Paule,

Your favourite play, of mine that is, was *A Life*, with *Summer* running it a close second. I recall that you all but clapped your hands with delight when I told you a few months ago that Ben Barnes was reviving it at the Abbey. This morning the tapes went up; we met in the rehearsal room high above Lower Abbey Street and had our read-through.

Where grief is concerned, there are trip-wires along the way and dangerous corners to be taken. Some of these such as birthdays, anniversaries, New Years and Christmas are foreseeable. The worst, however, are the unexpected moments that lie in ambush, and today's reading was so warm and sad and funny that, suddenly realising you would not be with me on the first night, I felt the author's all-purpose smile freeze and stiffen on my face like a plaster mask.

The two young girls of the play – a Fiona and a Fidelma – actually became the characters they were depicting; much as, in days of yore, the great F. J. Mc-Cormick could quite vanish into the skin of a Fluther Good, a Harold Mahony or a Faustus Kelly. They had the raw and bruised vulnerability of youth, the pristine ideals and the unawareness of the dragons that were lying in wait.

You, who always had the measure of great acting and were never fooled by bombast and fustian, would have seen your younger self in them and perhaps have cried a little. The day was not over, for I had been invited on board the P. & O. cruise liner, *Victoria*, moored at the North Wall on her way to Iceland and Norway. Seventeen years ago, as the *Sea Princess*, she was our first cruise ship, where we met Derek and Sheelagh Stevens, who were to become our close friends.

We took many a voyage on the *Princess*, some across the Atlantic to the West Indies, and one – the best of all – down the China Sea from Tientsin to Pusan, Nagasaki, Shanghai and Hong Kong. And yet what I remember most vividly is not a sea voyage at all, but an overland trip by Orient Express from Munich to Istanbul. It had been a not uneventful journey. There was the Incident of the Trousers which like the *Giant Rat of Sumatra* is, in the words of Dr Watson, 'a story for which the world is not yet prepared'.

Then the Bulgarian border guards burst into our compartment at 2 a.m. and a flashlight was shone on you in the top berth. 'Is this vumman your vife?' I was asked, and I replied in my best Marlene Dietrich accent: 'It took more than one man to change her name to Shanghai Lily.'

At Istanbul railway station, there was champagne, and we waltzed to a Viennese orchestra. When we emerged on to the quays it was to behold our beloved *Sea Princess* at her moorings in the Bosphorus as part of a cruise. It was like unexpectedly coming on a dear old friend, and you burst into tears of affection.

This evening there is a Lucullan dinner party given by the doughty sea-dog Captain Chris Sample and his lady, Veronica McSwiney. 'Why don't you come with us to the Eastern Med in September?' Vron urges. 'We'll look after you!' And, do you know, Paule, I have always wanted to see beautiful downtown Beirut, and I suddenly thought I just might do that. If you yourself had been with us this evening, you would have stowed away.

Wednesday

The devil has entered into me, for I am no sooner out of bed than I reserve a single cabin on board the *Victoria* for late September, when Veronica will join the vessel at Thessaloniki as the resident pianist. Then, with the mood still upon me, I go into town and buy a summery jacket. At my age, this is rather like an old maid slipping a crushed-up Viagra into the milkman's cuppa.

I have learned to fear these 'highs' of mood, for the trough that always follows is as dark as the blackest night. Letters keep coming in, but of course no one can really help. And there are tragedies: some bereaved people are still in mourning thirty years on. This morning I was much cheered, however, by condolences from our greatest diva, Bernadette Greevy, who quoted Thomas More writing to his daughter on the eve of execution: 'Pray for me, and I shall pray for you and your friends that we all may merrily meet in heaven.'

There are those, however, who insist that all deaths, yours included, are acts of God, and that I was spared for a divine purpose. I might agree with Alexander Pope that God takes note of the fall of a sparrow, which is not quite the same thing as suggesting that it was He who knocked the sparrow off its twig in the first place. In a play, I once wrote of a certain kind of Irish populism: 'They thank God for a fine day and stay diplomatically silent when it rains.'

No, what killed you was not a quixotic Deity saying 'Come in, Paule, your time is up!' and taking you unto Himself. It was asthma, helped by other things, such as an unsuspectedly frail heart, cigarettes ('I'm only a social smoker!' was your theme song) and a dogged insistence on doing housework that someone else could have come and done for you. And what left me alive and stupidly trying to find a purpose for continuing, was not any kind of divine plan. Rather, given my deplorable habits, it was a fluke which time will put smartly to rights a day, a week or a year hence.

I recall that once on a cruise you discovered that

one of the poker machines in the ship's casino was free and asked me to hold on to it while you fetched your store of American twenty-five cent pieces from our state-room. So I fed the machine, and when you returned I had eight quarters left. 'I'll just get rid of these,' I said and put them into the slot all at once. A royal flush came up and I won $750. You read me the riot act, then, and I can hear you doing so now for not going first, saying that there is no fairness under the sun. Too bloody true.

And one nice lady, an old friend of ours, wrote to say that she is saddened whenever, to quote J. K. Galbraith, I use my column 'not only to comfort the afflicted, but to afflict the comfortable'. She had no idea but perhaps she will have henceforth that it was you who most gleefully egged me on. I still recall that laugh of yours, the dirtiest in Christendom.

Thursday

Feeling the need to take Danielle to dinner at *Leiths* in Notting Hill, I call up the Pembridge Court Hotel in W.11 and book a room ten days hence. The petite, darkling manageress, Valerie Gilliatt, is certain to ask after you, Paule, so I leave word that there has been bereavement and it is not to be talked about. An hour later, Valerie calls.

If Grenfelling were a sport, this lady could do it for England. 'Darling, what nonsense this is and we'll have none of it,' she says crisply. 'I shall see you here at six o'clock on the nineteenth, and give you a very, *very* large Scotch!' This kindness, from the heart of heartless London, knocks me out.

Death, I have come to realise, is a kind of Irish bull. A wife dies, and the husband keeps asking why she isn't here to enjoy the tributes no one would have paid her had she been alive.

Friday

A call from Patrick Mason and Dame Ingrid Craigie in Singapore. It is late evening there, and my play has just finished its first performance; so the cast and director are knocking back gin slings in *Raffles Hotel*, lucky devils, and I wonder why I did not become an actor and be paid to trot the globe. I mention this over the phone to Danielle, and she says that I would have been a very bad actor, saying 'Rhubarb, rhubarb!' and living in a garret, upstairs from David Norris. What a supportive child you reared.

My evening is less exotic and consists of having a private dinner in a public place. The place is *The Vico* in Dalkey, which now has to be the best restaurant south of *L'Ecrivain*. My guest and I talk of life, death, elephants and poker. I learn a few things, one of which is that if you are a priest and play poker on a Good Friday, you are fated to end up with four queens, matched against someone else's four kings. Also, I learn, and it sticks in my mind like a burr, that the late Cardinal Basil Hume once said: 'Trying to pray is in itself prayer.'

I walk home afterwards and watch *Frasier*. This was the end of the current series, and it was a gobsmacker, for in the last ten seconds Daphne ran off with Niles on her wedding morn. I could almost hear your whoop of delight from beside me on the sofa.

And in today's *London Times* a hackette named Caitlin Moran – yes: Irish, I'm afraid – attempts to perform an enfeebled hatchet job on *Frasier*. It is more jeer than criticism and hardly worthy of comment except to remark on the space it wastes in a good newspaper. Also, one reflects that yet another untalented wannabe has tried to give herself stature by whittling her betters down to her own size.

Saturday

On 28 April 1789, Captain William Bligh, with eighteen men, was cast adrift from *HMS Bounty* in a 23-foot boat and made the 3,618-mile journey to Timor in 47 days. The four young lads who set sail from Bullock Harbour to New York fifty years ago today performed a comparable feat, and, unlike Bligh, they did it on purpose.

The voyage took 19 weeks, with stop-overs at Brest, Madeira, Las Palmas and Bermuda, and the accuracy of the landfalls must be accounted as a miracle of navigation. Our dear friend, Kevin O'Farrell, is the only survivor of the four and is present today when a handsome and almost vandal-proof bench was dedicated on the harbour quay. He is known these days as the Burgomaster of Killaloe, having gone to live there when (he says) it was so small a place that the population had to take it in turn to be the village idiot. The speechifying is done by the well-known historian and Sinn Féin hagiographer, Tim Pat Coogan.

Later, on television, I am enjoying an aria sung by Leslie Garrett and am reminded of a previous performance three or four months ago, when the domestic conversation went as follows:

Paule: Isn't she fantastic! Who is she?

Jack: Name of Leslie Garrett.

Paule: I never heard of her.

Jack (smugly): Yes, you did. I played one of her CDs in the car and you told me you couldn't abide her screeching and would I turn it off?

To which you made no reply, but gave me one of your James Finlayson looks (he was the bald squinty-eyed nemesis of Laurel and Hardy) that said you would get you own back. And, as usual, you did.

Love,
Jack

10

Dear Paule,

I saw none other than our one-time US ambassador, Mrs Jean Kennedy Smith, in *The Unicorn* at lunch-time and, by a miracle of self-restraint, merely smiled and said hello, managing not to observe in the manner of George S. Kaufman: 'Ah, forgotten but not gone!'

My luncheon guest, whom I have dubbed the Invisible Man, was talking to me about you and asked in his breaking-and-entering way if I were angry. I told him no. Then, as we walked out into a balmy summer's day of which in an untimely manner you had been robbed, I changed my mind. Yes, I *was* angry. At whom, though?

It dawns on me that I should get out more. *Medea* is on my list and Fiona Shaw is the best piece of uncured ham since Bette Davis. I long to see it, but am not so certain about the Stephen Rea production of *The Plough and the Stars*, which is returning to the Gaiety and might send the blood-pressure soaring beyond the recall of an o-d. of Betabloc. An anti-nationalist play set in 1916 has, so my friend Emer tells me, been updated and embellished as an anti-Brit polemic. One can guess what Sean O'Casey would have thought and said.

Somehow, and irrelevant as it may seem, I think about a letter which the Green Crow sent to Cyril Cusack forty years ago. A record company – Columbia, I think – had issued *Juno and the Paycock* on two LPs, but had truncated it so that the final scene between the Captain and Joxer was missing. O'Casey exploded. He wrote, 'God damn the ignorant bastards who know more about a play than he who wrote it!'

Mr Rea was probably wetting his nappy in an orange box – oh the irony! – and sucking on a comforter at that time, so I really cannot say why the thought comes into my head. I get scatty. This evening, when Gladys, our tortoiseshell, was not home by midnight, I set the alarm clock for 1 a.m., got up when it went off, padded downstairs and let her in. Barmy as I am, I don't think I would set an alarm for Mr Rea.

Tuesday

It is two murderous months ago today since you went, and a reader has very kindly sent me C. S. Lewis' *A Grief Observed*, published by Faber. His love affair with and marriage to an American divorcee named Joy Gresham was the basis for a most affecting play and a less good film called *Shadowlands*. I recall that I was so moved – wrecked is a better word – by the play and the acting that the star, Jane Lapotaire, became one of the only three actors – other than chums – to whom I was ever impelled to write a note of admiration. (She replied most graciously. The other two, Robert Lindsay and John Thaw, whom you, Paule, used to feed when he was young and hard up, responded not at all.)

Lewis' wife died of bone cancer, and his book – scribblings in four notebooks – is his attempt to come to terms with the pain of loss. Until today, I believed that any one person's grief was unique and had nothing at all in common with any other, so that there were no easy formulae, no lifelines which one could grasp for comfort. And yet in my own case at least two of Lewis' perceptions hit home.

He says that when one is happy, God is present all about one, and 'You will be welcomed with open arms. But go to Him when your need is desperate, when all other help is vain, and what do you find? A door slammed in your face, and a sound of bolting and double bolting on the inside. After that, silence.' Oh, that rings very true, and I begin to see, even if Lewis could not, what God is at.

Also, he says: 'I cannot see her face distinctly in my imagination. No doubt the explanation is simple enough. We have seen the faces of those we know best so variously, from so many angles, with so many expressions waking, sleeping, laughing, crying, eating, talking, thinking that all the impressions crowd into our memory together and cancel out in a mere blur. But her voice is still vivid.' Spot on.

Wednesday

My father, bless him, never journeyed farther from home than on a Mystery Tour to Kilkenny and once with my mother to visit us when we lived outside Manchester. And yet, on coming out of doors on a summer evening, he would look at a mackerel sky and observe: 'Isn't this the best bloody country in the world!'

If he had said 'most beautiful', I might not have disagreed. But 'best'? Are you, for instance, aware, my dear, that until today you were not dead, because, to someone in the toxicological department of a hospital you were never a person, but only a specimen on a slide to be analysed and dealt with when the humour should take. Alas, the said humour has not yet taken and so, for more than two months, there is still no death certificate.

I asked and asked; and the coroner's office referred me to the doctor who performed the post mortem (which was necessary because you died at home and without a doctor present), and that doctor pointed me towards a blank wall of hospital labs and departments in Beaumont and St James. Meanwhile, the three of us, you, Danielle and I, existed in limbo, where your death was frozen in time because nobody thought of you as a person.

Finally, the Deputy Coroner, Dr Breathnach called me today and, most kind man that he is, solved the great mystery. You died of bronchial asthma, and at last now you can rest. Hallelujah!

Of course there are those who are worse off. I keep thinking of a tourist who, as I write, is fighting for life in an intensive care unit. The reason is, some say, that a Holiday Inn was built smack in the middle of Pearse Street, which, after dark, is one of the city's no-go areas. (What a stupid remark, when the city at large is a no-go area.) Or no; perhaps it served the man right, because the reprobate had a black wife, and, the cheek of them, they walked our streets with their coffee-coloured offspring.

In his column in the *Irish Crimes*, Kevin Myers goes so far off the rails on the subject as to constitute a one-man Tay Bridge disaster. He blames, wait for it, the dearth of night-time taxis. He says nothing at all about what might befall people who cannot afford the price of a taxi, even if there was one around, or a late bus for that matter, or if a person perhaps minced as he walked along. And nothing is said, either, about the virtual non-policing in a low-life area, or a certain notorious pub that exists cheek by jowl with a tourist hotel, or the gangs of knife-wielding gutties that are allowed to roam unhindered.

All of these were factors in the butchery. They were an end-product of what can be summed up in the great, dismissive, let's feck-off-home Irish philosophy of 'Ah, sure it'll do.' What will happen now is that a garda presence in Pearse Street will be stepped up for three weeks, then another outrage elsewhere will shove this one on to the back burner, and it will be a case of as-you-were. And of course Bertie will, as usual, do bugger all, because tourists do not have votes.

Our politics, national and local are a quagmire of corruption. It is a legacy of a peasant culture that back-handers and bribes are seen as a normal, even desirable, way of life. The real tragedy is that all the rabblement from Haughey down, or nowadays from Haughey up, see no harm at all in their sleaze. Fianna Fáil was founded and still exists on an unspoken – except at an Ard Fheis, perhaps – concept of a master race to whom all thing are permitted by way of privilege.

The same neo-fascist attitude enabled the Catholic hierarchy to move perverted priests from one parish to another, rather than expose them or even kick their ordained arses in private. Brendan Smith and his kind were thus enabled to prey on new victims because the Church was always held to be more important than raped children. Any clique is self-protective and self-perpetuating, right down to *Aosdána*, a harmless little bunch of bogus elitists to whom knowing their artistic arse from elbow comes down the field.

'The best bloody country? Da, do me a favour. The Celtic Tiger, poor beast, should be humanely put down.'

(By the way, Paule, is there laughter in heaven? Your passing was mourned by the President and reported on RTE and in the national press. It did not, however, rate a mention in either the *Skibbereen Eagle* or the *Dalkey Newsletter*. So hang up your halo.)

Thursday

The great and good Tom Mythen has invited me to lunch at the *King Sitric*, so I simply catch a DART to Howth, and there is a wonderful meal at the end of it. In a good, a very good sense of the phrase, this was truly the piece of cod that passeth all understanding.

All day yesterday where you were concerned, I had the dreaded black dog for company. The least thing could trigger it: a dry-cleaning tag pinned to a garment, or – and farce keeps breaking in – a pair of underpants folded and put away inside out, maybe this was a manifestation of your left-handedness.

Also, you mangled the English that was, after all, not your native tongue. Over lunch today, I heard you telling me, as you frequently did: 'If you don't eat those vegetables, you're going to catch curfew!'

It is nice to be reminded that a restaurant as good and as lightsome as the *King Sitric* is at the end of an hour's train ride from across the bay. And Tom, nice man that he is, has invited Dan and me to the Wexford Opera in October. He even suggests that I bring a 'floozy'. The floozy-queue is hereby urged to form to the right.

Friday

I am a trial and vexation to my friends. One caring and much-loved lady – who I suspect, does not approve of these letters to you – says that I am destroying myself with grief and urges me to snap out of it. She suggests that I go for long brisk walks – is she trying to kill me? – but stops short, bless her, at cold showers.

All is not dismal, however. In Boswell's *The Life of Samuel Johnson* there is an utterance from the lawyer, Oliver Edwards: 'I have tried, too, in my time to be a philosopher; but, I don't know how, cheerfulness was always breaking in'. So it is with me, although the cheerfulness is these days thin on the ground.

The other day, I had a luncheon appointment with a charming young lady, and she suggested that we meet at the gate of the People's Park in Dun Laoghaire. Later, during my now nightly call to Danielle in London I said: 'Can you imagine when I last waited for a girl at a park gate?' At this, she laughed for at least 40p. worth of off-peak telephone call.

I must go, for Panache needs grooming. For want of tlc, he is beginning to look like an explosion in an eiderdown factory.

Love,
Jack

11

Dear Paule,

Some months ago, I wrote that the worst part of living alone is not the loneliness – all writers are lonely; it's why we write – but the aloneness. There is a difference. After your death, I discovered that I had always been a natural sharer. I dislike eating alone or going to the cinema on my own, and I hate looking at television without someone at the other end of the sofa.

In my mind, I still live with you. And no, it is not an obsession; I don't talk to you or to myself, either, but last week, for example, I watched a video-tape of *The Talented Mr Ripley* and could almost hear you saying 'This is brutal!' which was your ultimate Depart-from-Me verdict, beyond reprieve. I could not agree more: it was indeed interminable and 'brutal'.

Recently, a lady of our acquaintance finally washed her hands of her rogue of a husband, and when I met her casually in the town, I wished that you had been present, for you would have thrown your arms around her and insisted on our taking her to dinner. And, a few years ago, when another man walked out on his wife, both of them friends of ours, we made a solemn pact that we would stay neutral and not take sides. Of course the word 'impartial' was not in your dictionary. Later that very same day, you came storming in from your shopping with 'Do you know what the little bastard has done now?'

Your list of *bêtes noires* was endless: it included Marlon Brando ('A mumbler!'), all of Shakespeare (and shame on you!), especially *Hamlet* (and hurrah for you!), coloratura sopranos, cleverness, most westerns, all war films, Dietrich's singing, Stallone or Schwarzenegger or Steiger doing *anything*, and what you called 'films with venetian blinds, ceiling fans and sweaty men in vests'. Oh yes, and being obliged to wear a skirt instead of slacks. Trousers, you would say, were the only useful thing that men ever invented.

(And, by the way, you loved *A Little Night Music, Moonstruck, The Shop Around the Corner, The Music Man, Gigi*, Bette Davis, all animals (snap!), *Heartbeat, A Touch of Frost, Poirot*, Anthony Hopkins, Laurel and Hardy, Utrillo and Renoir, the *Antiques Roadshow*, cryptic crosswords and poker, poker, poker!)

What the foregoing rigmarole is about is that this evening I watched a thing called *It's the Wrong Answer*, on RTE. It was a quiz show with, as usual, a young compere who could not afford a necktie and who believed in common with everyone else in RTE that 'films' was a two-syllable word and that 'water' and 'matter' were pronounced as 'waw-her' and 'mah-her'.

At one point, however, he actually said of a contestant: 'He's a horticulturist. Which means he didn't get a green finger from picking his nose.'

I am not making this up; true as God, that is what he said. This, for once and at long last, was not something I would have wished to share with you. I cried 'Faughhh!' in disgust and would have made a run for the bathroom, only you were in there ahead of me. While I was waiting for my turn, I did call up Danielle in London. 'Do you know what I just heard on RTE?' I said, and told her.

'Tasteless,' she said enigmatically.

Tuesday

I have lunch with a nice lady from the Abbey on the subject of my conducting what she laughingly describes as a master class in play-writing. She is taken aback – shocked even – on learning that you and I allowed The Pooka, Gladys and Panache on the bed at night, and, as you must be aware, I still do. Actually, one would hardly know they are they there, except that Panache sleeps across my ankles, stopping the blood flow and causing my toes to drop off from gangrene.

As of yore, the other two arrive at about 7 a.m. They seem to have an instinct for when my sleep is becoming shallow, and they move in accordingly. If it is close to getting-up time, Gladys, who misses you, comes and snoozes in the hollow of my throat and sticks her whiskers up my nose. The Pooka climbs on my chest and stares me in the face until I both give up and get up.

First, however, Panache gets off the bed, stands on the floor and, with needle-like claws, gives me five minutes of exquisite acupuncture. He is otherwise the gentlest of the three except that he is long-haired and needs grooming. Today I take a comb and a brush to him, and he stretches and purrs with undisguised lust. His chest resembles the fluffy shirt of a Mississippi gambler, and he takes such erotic pleasure in the experience that I feel like the madam of an upmarket Bullock Harbour brothel.

Wednesday

In town, and as many people do nowadays, a man from Galway stops me to express sympathy for my 'trouble'. With references to a bereavement of his own, he quotes what to him was a comforting line from my book *Home Before Night*, which I interpolated into *Da* for the Broadway production. It is 'Love turned upside down is love for all that.'

I recall that during the previews, an Irishwoman wrote in extreme anger to the *New York Times*, saying that love turned upside down was not love at all, but hatred. This threw the producers into a panic. Their microdot of faith in the play evaporated in an instant. What, they demanded, were we to do about this woman's terrible letter to the *Times*? How could we now survive?

Bemused, I replied that it was only one person's opinion and that any publicity was good publicity. Then the producer-in-chief, Lester Osterman (you spoonerised him as Oster Lesterman) looked at me and said: 'You're a crazy Irishman, you know that? With your attitood, we're gonna die like dogs!'

After the first night and the standing ovation, I said 'Woof-woof' into his ear, but I doubt if he ever got the point. And yes, love turned upside down was, and is, love for all that. We, you and I, ought to know.

Thursday

Do you remember Ming? He was, and still is, a brother of The Pooka and is sleek and seal-dark. I gave him as a gift to your friend, Joan who called him Ming because she had never seen *Flash Gordon*, and three months ago he disappeared and was widely mourned. Sightings were reported around dustbins at a school a mile off, but knowing what school lunches are like, the banner of hope flew at half mast.

You will be delighted to know that this week the truant was discovered by a lady who delivered him to a local vet, and that he is now at home in a somewhat slimmed-down version, but as contented a mog as you will find west-nor'west of The Pooka, Gladys and Panache.

The only sadness is that three months in a cat's life is the equivalent of seven times as long for a human. So poor Ming has missed at least one Christmas.

Friday

This afternoon, I came home from the supermarket and, for no reason at all, remembered a dream I had about you last night; so I sat down among the cat-meat and the jacket from the dry cleaners and wept. And no, it was not a dream either, but a memory of one night three years ago when we were on the river Charente. It is my favourite stream, just north of Bordeaux, and you were wearing a knee-length, ivory-coloured *crepe-de-Chine* night-dress.

Two of our guests had decided that a French river was not for them, and had found a quarrelsome pre-text to abandon ship the following day. Rather than have a row, I had gone to bed, and you, assuming that I was already asleep, came in, bent down and kissed me lovingly on the forehead. It was your unshakeable belief that if anyone was going to be abusive to me, it would be yourself and no one else. And so, remembering this, I cried, but from happiness for the first time since 13 April.

Thank you.
Love,
Jack

12

Dear Paule,

Like everyone else, you and I doted on *Casablanca*, and I can still hear you chuckle at the bit of existentialist chat between Bogart and his French *poule*, played by Madeleine Le Beau who was more fun, one would have thought, than Ingrid ('Was that cannon fire, or is it my heart pounding?') Bergman. The little two-step went as follows:

Yvonne: Where were you last night?

Rick: That's so long ago, I don't remember.

Yvonne: Will I see you tonight?

Rick: I never make plans that far ahead.

Well, ever since you left me and went off into the stars at virtually no notice, I don't make plans either, not unless it is for something like a Terry Keane evening of ecdysiastics and exotic dance for which one is obliged to reserve a hair-shirt and a blindfold six months in advance. Nonetheless, I am going to leap headlong to the year's end and prophesy that Mary Harney will win the *Gobshite of the Year* trophy, not only outright but with oak leaf cluster.

The Haughey business was as hilarious as the German officer in *Dad's Army* asking Ian Lavender 'Vat iss your name?' and Arthur Lowe saying 'Don't tell him, Pike!' Not that it matters: they would never have sent Champagne Charlie to the hoosegow anyway – not even to that open prison in Kinsealy. They might have given him a smack on the wrist and sentenced him to do community service – kissing Mrs H. once a day, perhaps – but, as regards serving time, the Pope would be more likely to turn up in Mecca saying: 'Young people of Islam, I loff you!'

Convicted or not, Chas the Chancer will in any case go down to posterity as lower in the public esteem than the unshaven panhandler who catches one's arm in the street and begs for 'Twenty p. for a cuppa tay, boss.' He is for ever rubbished: a verruca on the sole of history. As a team, however, I can see the burgeoning of a new comedy act called Haughey and Harney – think of Stan and Olly – with Harney, covered in custard pies and opprobrium, saying to her partner: 'Why don't you do something *to* help me?'

(And we could have a scene with the pair in a holiday caravan, as in *Them Thar Hills*. Harney would be at the stove, cooking. Haughey would say: 'What's for dinner, Olly?' and receive the magisterial reply: 'Coffee and beans, Stanley.' To which the reply would come from little Haughey: 'Gee, you sure know how to plan a meal!' Who says that great comedy is dead?

Nonetheless, full marks to Ms Hardy sorry – I

mean Harney – who dived in, leaving Haughey to warble 'Mary is a grand old dame'. It just goes to prove that to be a senior politician you need to be either as crooked as a ram's horn or as thick as a Mountjoy sandwich. And Ms Harney is as honest as a summer's day is long.

Tuesday

Like Ado Annie in *Oklahoma!* 'I'm jist a gurl who caint say no', and I rashly agreed to be interviewed on the Marian Finucane radio show. I knew it was regarded as a big deal when my minder at RTE kept standing between me and the toilet door – interviewees, I was told, have been known to lock themselves in. In the event, I could not have been in kindlier hands – Marian is a lovely lady – and I emerged like a man who walks away from a car crash with mere bruises.

Later, at the Savoy cinema, there is a preview of *Mission: Impossible – 2*, which should have been renamed *Mission: Impertinent*. I was in the mood for some good old-fashioned, stylish trash, but this proved to be a gigantic ego trip for Tom Cruise, a kind of outsized midget with the personality of wet Kleenex. It is a vast, featureless Gobi Desert of a film, inspired by slavering greed and utterly devoid of wit or invention.

There were rubbery facemasks which changed the wearer's identity and were put on faster than one could say 'This is crap.' And there were yawnnnnn and zzzzzzz car chases. Computer graphics enabled Mr Cruise to joust on a motor cycle, and there was even the ending with hair on it, where you think the villain is dead, but up he comes, just begging, to quote O'Casey's Juno, 'to be made a colander of'.

Anthony Hopkins, no less, was in it like a begging ass for two scenes – brief and uncredited, but, presumably, paid for – and Brendan Gleason put his career in pawn as a blubbering cretin in what we used to call the Gene Lockhart role. However, nobody except wee Tom was given a look in, and the farrago had as much style as could be wedged into a gnat's navel, with enough space left over for a Malteser.

It was all about a virus that Threatened to Destroy the World, and if I were infected with it I would first of all go and breathe on Tom Cruise. Four or five people applauded at the end and were instantly put down humanely by a member of the SPCA. So, yet another two hours of my life have been wasted, and one can only agree with the pithy summation of the *New Yorker* magazine, which said: 'M: I – 2 is N: f-ing: G'.

Wednesday

'Violence', as Alan Brien observed, 'is the repartee of the illiterate'. Today, a letter – no sender's address given (of course!) – says in its entirety: 'Hugo, if you snarl at me again I will give you a fast boxing lesson followed by my KO punch. See you on the Metals, Bucko.' It was signed: 'Jack Coffey, Nonpareil.' The Metals is a laneway that runs from Dalkey to Dun Laoghaire, but I have no idea who or what a Jack Coffey Nonpareil is or why I should have wasted one of my snarls on him or it.

I never hit even nonpareil children, except when no one is looking, but I'll send my daughter to the Metals. Pistols for two, ice-lollies for one (dear God, it's like living in a John Ford western).

No matter; today I meet the Abbey cast of *A Life* for lunch and a walk to Sorrento Park, where part of the play is set. Dalkey is a haunting place, filled with ghosts; the names veer between Italianate (Vico, Sorrento, Nerano) and reminders of Empire (Victoria, Kalafat, Trafalgar and Khyber Pass). The granite-topped park itself – a remnant of the Commons of Dalkey, which were an uncertain refuge at a time of plague – is a granite outcrop at the point where the two bays, Dublin and Killiney, meet.

Today, I recalled that my mother used to sit, her back to the gorse, with other old ones, facing the view that might have been the Bay of Naples in reverse, with the Sugar Loaf as its modest Vesuvius. At the Ramparts, just up the way, I would look on fearfully as my father, stripped to his pelt, dived from the rocks into the sea, and our dog, Jack, swam rings round him.

In the park itself, Des Collier and I played cowboys in what we called the box canyon. I always played the villain Douglas Dumbrille or Morris Ankrum because one got to grimace, pivot like a dervish and bite the dust. It was not Dalkey then, it was Illyria.

And high on a rock-face there is a mosaic 'portrait' of the lute-playing John Dowland, who supposedly was a friend of Shakespeare's. Before its formal unveiling, one of our gang climbed up the rock face to peer under the cloth that covered it. 'What's it like?' we asked. He said, disgustedly: 'It's only an oul nun playin' the banjo.'

Thursday

To *Brownes* on Stephen's Green for lunch, and on a summer's day the chicken salad is, as they say, to die for. My guest dares not imbibe, so I have a half-bottle of an Alsatian wine: the celebrated *Gestrantzenmatzenubergruppensturm-fuhrer*. 'You look good,' my guest says, meaning it. 'Far better than you did a month ago.' My voice gives a hypochondriacal quiver. 'Why? How did I look then?'

'Your eyes were dead in your head.'

And it is true. I am at last over the shock of having seen 45 years with you wiped out in an instant. After eleven weeks of the horrors, I can accept that you are gone. Which, of course, only increases the feeling of loss and the endlessness of grief. I still turn to watch you smile at a joke we might have shared, only to find you not there. I wonder if I dare allow The Pooka to stay out past midnight, or if I might buy a garment without risking your derision. Today – and there is surely mirth in Elysium – I went into *Monaghans* and bought a pair of cotton trousers that convert to shorts in the twinkling of a zip. If the idea of me swanning about in shorts doesn't bring you back to haunt me, nothing ever will.

And I recall all the madnesses: how we once took two infuriated sea-crabs to the pictures at the Adelphi, Dun Laoghaire, never mind why, and how they escaped, crazed further by Greer Garson in *Madame Curie*, and how I hunted them down the aisle, and recaptured them where they had fetched up against the base of the screen. I caused a near-riot by calling to you for a thousand cinemagoers to hear: 'Paule, I have the crabs!'

(The self-same crustaceans walked back into the sea at Sandymount later that evening, inspiring Zero Mostel to give an impression of one crab meeting another on the sea-bed: 'Hey, I was at this movie last evening. It was called *Bambi*, and it was all about this ****ing deer!')

And only six months ago, as you and I were setting off for the theatre, you actually asked me 'Should we leave a light on for the cats?' and I replied: 'Do you think they might want to read?' The laughter after *that* remark lasted us all the way past Glenageary and as far as the Widow Gamble's Hill.

No, the grief and the missing will never end, at

least not until I do, but these letters must, soon. It is getting on for time that I stood up straight and walked unaided. There have been so many letters, cards, books, prayers and even, from my friend Colette in Cyprus, an audio tape featuring 'Paule's Song' which I have not the courage to listen to. Only today, a letter which took three scrawled pages to tell me to 'Snap out of it' arrived in my local pub. For all its fearless finger-wagging, it was left cravenly unsigned, so I spiked it in the wc for a needy person to use.

People write to me, superbly confident that you are in heaven. And yet, despite their certainty, they could not even say if there are chairs there or if one has to stand or kneel for all eternity. These people merely *hope* and call it faith. And here on earth these months past hopefully, foolishly, childishly – my antennae have been alert for a hint, the merest whisper of a sign that you are around in spirit. Alas, nothing. Mind, your favourite potted plant, which has spiked leaves of green and blood red, has just flowered with new lilac-coloured buds.

Meanwhile, I am 'managing'. As regards caring for myself, I have two Delia Smith cook books in the kitchen, and if ever push comes to shove I can put them in the microwave and eat them. After my play opens at the Abbey, I shall write you a final letter, then go and meet Danielle, who will be taking your place as first mate on a canal in the far east of France.

As one finds grief easier to endure with each week that passes, there is a sense of shame and betrayal. One clings to death as if it were a mistress no longer loved and yet whom one cannot brutally discard. And how paradoxical it is that the further in time one gets from the experience itself, the more chilling and unbearable it becomes to dwell upon.

Perhaps it is just that I cannot suffer ever to think of you in the past tense. So, very much for the present.

Love,
Jack

13

Dear Paule,

I spoke to only two people all day today. One was Danielle on the telephone and the other was an Italian waiter at the bistro, *Ragazzi*, up the town. And even he would not have spoken to me had he known that France was just about to score that goal in extra time.

Since you left, you have haunted my thoughts, but you spared my dreams. Tonight, however, I dreamt I was in a strange house packing to go home, but was unable to find you when the time came to leave. Finally, I managed to telephone a doctor, who said most cheerfully that you were in hospital having 'a bone removed' and would be restored to me in two weeks.

As The Pooka nestled on my chest at 7.30 a.m. as usual, I was trying (in my dream) to decide whether I should go home on my own or stay with my parents in our two-roomed slum cottage – long demolished now – in Kalafat Lane. Sigmund Freud would have had a ball with this one.

Monday
A lady e-mails me to say that I rudely passed her in the

street without returning her greeting. I should smile at people, she tells me, and that would please *you* no end. I reply apologetically, telling her what is true, that I am both shy and slightly deaf. The thought of beaming at strangers on the road, as if I were a village idiot, appals me.

Apropos of this, I remember chairing a press conference when I was Programme Director of the Dublin Theatre Festival. Espying the journalist, Mary Holland, whom I had not already met but knew by sight, I went over and said 'You're welcome'. To which Ms Holland replied, coldly: 'And do you think I should know you?' At which this blushing violet wilted and retired, permanently, to his window box.

The next time I saw Ms Holland was years later at the Gate Theatre, when she came up and said that she was enjoying my play very much (it was an adaptation of *A Tale of Two Cities*). Guess what my witty reply was? I said 'Thank you.' But, like Bertie Wooster when he said 'Good morning' to Jeeves', I intended it to sting.

I am not bothered that my correspondent believes me to be a curmudgeon, scowling at people who smile on the street – it is always easier to cling to a wrong opinion than to form a new one. What I find irksome is the suggestion that you, Paule, are Up There, with nothing better to do than monitor my behaviour through some kind of celestial telescope. Probably you are thought of as being transparent, like a Hollywood ghost who wears a white nightshirt and walks through walls. What drivel people believe in!

Also, lurking in my mailbag like an adder in a strawberry bed, is the following, with no address, but a Cork postmark. The text in full is: 'Dear Jack, You asked recently did I love you. The answer is no. Sure a mother wouldn't have you. She gave you away and you became a bastard only boy. Love *Paule*.'

My dearest Paule, I love my country well, I like bits of it, but would somebody kindly point out the nearest exit – apart, that is, from ten Nemutals and/or a bottle of Scotch?

Tuesday

And as if in answer to that last question, there comes a letter of a very different kind from our old friend, the actress Mia Dillon, in New York. She was the 'Yellow Peril' in *Da* on Broadway, and I recall escorting her to the Tony Awards that year as my date. *Da* had been nominated for four gongs, including Best Play, and in the taxi Mia said: 'One day, I'm going to get a Tony of my own, but until that happens this will do!'

I had deliberately not invited you to come to New York with me. If I hadn't won a Tony – and I knew that at that time no Irish writer had ever done so – I would have shrugged and pretended it was no matter and better luck next time. But you were the one person I could never fool. You would have taken one look at my false smile, smiled back at me, and privately cursed the judges and New York for ever.

Well, as it happened, there was no need; we bagged four Tonys. Now Mia says she is still acting and, as of last year, is happily married; also, she has a degree in Oriental Medicine and is a licensed acupuncturist. She asks me to come to New York soon, 'where you'll be surrounded by people who love you.' Well, that would be nice, always supposing that my fan clubs, including the one in Cork, can get on without me.

Wednesday

I have hardly awoken when inspiration strikes. Danielle and I had planned in a half-hearted way to spend Christmas in Madeira, but no sooner am I out of bed than this fixture has been scratched. Instead I go mad and book two Concorde tickets to New York, departing from Heathrow on 23 December at 10.30 a.m. and arriving at JFK at 9.20. Hump the begrudgers, and, as James Cagney observed in *The Strawberry Blonde*, that's the kind of hairpin I am.

A memory comes to me of the first time I flew by Concorde. I arrived in New York before mid-morning and checked into the Dorset Hotel, and I set off for a press conference wearing a suit of Donegal tweed, made to measure by Kevin and Howlin. A group of men were drinking coffee at a sidewalk café, and as I walked past they broke into a lusty chorus of 'When

Irish Eyes are Smiling'. I did a turn about, went back to the Algonquin, changed out of my suit and never wore it again.

And, years later, you and I were on a Concorde flight to Washington, DC, when President Reagan sacked the American air traffic controllers. We were on our approach to Dulles Airport, with the forests of West Virginia a green blur beneath our windows, when the captain made an announcement. With imperturbable British *sang froid*, he said: 'Ladies and gentlemen, the air traffic controllers have gone home rather earlier than we would have liked, but we'll endeavour to cope.' He performed a flawless landing by sight alone, and a hundred or so items of undergarments were never the same again.

Thursday
Up at 6.30 and to the airport to meet our dear friend, Joe Contino, who has come from Chicago to be with me on your account. My daughter and my friends, bless 'em, are the greatest argument I know against helping oneself to that cup of hemlock.

Joe's first wife died six years ago, just before I met him for the first time, and he tells me that her wish was to have her ashes scattered at Ravello in Italy. He brought the urn home from the crematorium and placed it, for the time being, on the mantelpiece of his living-room. He then opened the French windows, and there was suddenly a great wind not from outside the house, but from the room itself, blowing outwards.

He believed that her spirit was leaving, and I believe him. When Mrs Patrick Campbell died, the shadow of a great wing was seen to sweep across the room. In your case, and since you did nothing by halves; there would be either the gentlest zephyr or a hurricane that would blow me clear out to sea.

Joe has come bearing gifts: a 2-litre flagon of J&B, a new book entitled *In the Heart of the Sea*, about the whaling disaster that inspired *Moby Dick*, a framed photograph of you and me, and, being the Joe that he is, a half-dozen Viagras.

This evening, I go alone to the first preview of *A Life* at the Abbey. It is all I could wish for. The new lines, inserted last week, work a treat, and John Kavanagh and Stephen Brennan are an irresistible double-act. And yet, this play – your favourite – is another dark milestone to be passed.

You were always far too nervous to go to previews, and this is the first time I have not sped straight home afterwards to hear your two questions, unchanged down the years: 'How did it go?' and 'Were there many at it?' Instead, I call Danielle and give the answers to her instead, saying: 'It went superbly' and 'The house was all but full.' My life is an egg without salt. God, but I miss you.

And so I sit up late when my houseguest has gone

to bed and think of W. H. Auden, who wrote of a dead lover who had been:

My noon, my midnight, my talk, my song;
I thought that love would last for ever; I was wrong.

Friday

There is to be a new Irish political party. They are fated to be an instant shoo-in. Like, I suspect, the vast majority of people, I think that at this stage I would vote for Attila the Hun. About Saddam Hussein, I am still not so sure.

I buy a copy of *Harry Potter and the Goblet of Fire*, which is published today, and unblushingly tell my bookseller friend that it is for my granddaughter. Well, I do have a grand daughter – two words, that is. The last work of fiction I really enjoyed was *The Silence of the Lambs*, and I was learning French at the time at a school in Provence. You were with me, and I rationed you to 50 pages a day; so that while I was at morning classes, you enjoyed a lie-in – our bedroom was in an old mill overlooking poppy fields – and devoured the book, word by word.

I am so tired of arty-farty works of fiction that are critics' darlings and Booker bunkum. *The English Patient* all but caused me to put my jaw out from terminal boredom, and the endless film version was even worse. And William Trevor's tangential novels are as tedious as his short stories are perfect. How nice it will be to read *Harry Potter* for a change. In fact, I dip into it, and it is sloppily written and yet done with the excited breathlessness of the born storyteller who is carried away by his own lovely lies.

And if, on the very day this appears, I manage to get to Strasbourg and the canal that wends its crooked way through Alsace towards the Rhine, then I shall give *Harry Potter* to our grand daughter. Anyone who is too old to read a children's book is too old for all else.

Saturday

In town, I buy a few slim books as first night keepsakes for the cast, even though the play is not a new work but a revival. There is no recognised protocol on such occasions. A playwright friend of mine does no more than give his actors greeting cards. Another dramatist – a flinty Northerner – says in his fine Malone Road accent: 'Whay the hell should Ay give 'em onnything? Aren't the buggers being ped?' Mean sod.

At this evening's preview, to which I escort my godmother, Helen Lucy Burke, there are residents of Topeka, Kansas wherever one looks. I am seated behind a family of Americans who have come to the Abbey in the same spirit as one visits the Blarney Stone. They seem taken aback that the experience involves the chore of sitting through a play.

A teenaged son, as brawny as a prize bull, sprawls

and lolls and all but uproots his seat, banging it backwards into my knees. I snarl 'Stop that!' which fright-
ens him for a while. The play manages to exert a hold
on them during Act Two, and whenever there is a joke
and the audience responds, the question 'Why are they
laughing?' runs along their row like a prairie fire. What
a good time you would have had.

Love,
Jack

14

Dear Paule,

You are probably familiar with the phrase 'Going pub-lic.' Well, as of today, and as far as you are concerned, I am going private. No more soul-baring on this page; although in the practical sense, I must go on living in a cleft stick. By which I mean that while on the one hand, I am incapable of living alone, on the other I could not share a roof with anyone, nor could anyone live with me. Well, perhaps a saint could do so, which would be hell on earth for both of us.

I was always the most fortunate of mortals. I had a life's companion whose affection, wretch that I was, I took for granted, I did work that I loved and earned enough from it for travel and the odd splurge and to take friends to dinner.

And on Thursday next, the thirteenth, let triskai-dekaphobes beware! it will be 13 weeks to the day since another Thursday, 13 April, when the earth opened under me. You went in a moment. I begged you aloud: 'Don't die!' but it had already happened. These open letters helped me for a while, and maybe I shall drop you a line from France next week, but I had better get

131

on with the dismal business of living.

This week, I continue to have a house guest, Joe Contino, who suddenly said in the town today 'I need to find a good yarn!' I suggested that he either buy the new *Harry Potter* novel or read the typescript of my book, but it turned out that what he wanted was a length of stout cotton thread.

When he found it – and it was a bright fire-engine red – he knotted it into a kind of enormous tassel, which he then tied to the handle of my suitcase. He told me: 'I was once arrested for taking someone else's bag out of an airport by mistake. Now you'll recognise which case is yours when it comes up on the carousel.' He is full of such wheezes and, speaking of wheezing, washes the ashtray when he is finished smoking.

'Joanne and I don't smoke at home,' he tells me, seeing nothing incongruous about smoking in *my* home. But it behoves me to be tolerant, for I was once a 65-a-day man. Later, you were always quick to remind me of this when I dared to wave away the smoke from one of your all too presciently-named coffin nails. You protested that you were only a 'social' smoker. If so, then there was no end to your sociability.

(Americans are crazy people. They treat cigarette smokers like villainous carriers of the Black Death, and yet every home is a virtual arsenal, bulging with handguns. Babes, who from birth suck on the teated muzzles of .38 revolvers, are trained to perforate any callers who might come to the wrong address after nightfall. It means nothing to the spiritual heirs of Daniel Boone that in 1994 – I reach for a casual statistic – a whopping 12,769 people were killed by handguns in the United States.)

Tuesday

It seems that draconian new laws are to be enacted by way of making accountants pull their socks up and behave. 'Too late!' I hear you say, remembering the inimitable Charles Russell Murphy, who took us to the cleaners to the tune of £248,000. Our acquaintance, Gay Byrne, was robbed of less than a third of that amount, but more than made up for it in hollering.

About a fortnight before Russell died, he was negotiating on our behalf for the purchase of the apartment in which I write these words. When we first viewed the place, you shrugged and said, all but yawning, 'I would not mind living there.' This, in Paule-speak, could be translated as 'Oh, please, buy it for me. I would kill for it!'

I agreed to pay the asking price, and the vendor, knowing we were hooked, greedily upped it by £10,000, so Russell wrote to say that, rather than be intimidated, we should back off and forget about buying the place. You wailed: 'We're going to lose it!' That morning, as it happened, I was flying to London, and I called Russell from the airport, instructing him to meet the new price. I said: 'It's Paule's dream home, so please call her and say that all is well.'

He did so, there and then, and the last words he ever spoke to you in this world were 'You do trust me, don't you?' In spite of his roguery, we always liked Russell Murphy, but if they have money in heaven, please don't lend him any. Already, he has probably sold the Pearly Gates to a developer.

Wednesday
A female, at least the handwriting so suggests, gives her address simply as 'Ashford' and signs herself 'P' (for 'Paule'?). She is glad, she says, that I am giving up writing these 'silly' letters. Then she gets catty and her claws show. Her sentiments hardly bother me, but I marvel at the gutlessness of people who are afraid to sign their names and yet waste good money on a stamp and paper and ink. Nobody minds them. And yet, call it paranoia, if you will, but when packets of cat food arrived here anonymously last week, I binned the lot. You would have done no less.

Thursday
There are letters to be answered, perhaps a dozen, and nearly all are from people who are coping or not coping with bereavement of their own. Perhaps the most touching is from a man who says he sleeps on his late wife's side of the bed so that he will not have to look at

her empty pillow.

For myself, and in a strange way, I have never felt more married than I do at this moment, but there is a small regret that our story has been broken off before its proper ending. Life is a bad playwright, and the loose ends are still there, exposed and raw. One thinks of bits of unfinished business and how one vaguely thought that one day all the 't's would be crossed and the 'i's dotted.

Not so very long ago – during some small contretemps, I forget the context – you reproached me with 'I often think my friends know me better than you do.' It took a while for this to sink in, and when it did, I wanted to answer you. There is a phrase, *esprit descalier*, which describes all the clever remarks one thinks of on the way upstairs to bed: i.e., when it is too late for a riposte.

I would have told you, and not in any critical sense: 'But you show your friends an outward part of yourself, whereas what I get is the private you. I am not complaining; this is the you I prefer; but outsiders experience you at your best, whereas I see you in the round, at moments when you show tiredness or impatience or crossness, or whatever.'

By then, of course, the time for a response had gone past, and the argument, honed and, as I thought, unanswerable, stayed inside my head. Sleeping dogs were let lie, and now alas, they will never be awoken. Perhaps you died feeling misunderstood, but then so do most women, for there is no understanding them.

We think we have limitless time, and we don't. As John Greenleaf Whittier never quite wrote:

For all sad words of tongue or pen,
The saddest are these
I'll get around to it sometime.

Friday
Yesterday, my literary agent called and ask 'Are you sitting down?' After fourteen rejections, my first novel has been accepted and by a most reputable London house. How proud you would have been, but torturers with white-hot tongs could not have induced you to say so. I can almost hear you muttering that my opinion of myself is high enough as it is.

When I had it finished, I gave the typescript to you and suggested that you read it at the rate of sixty pages a day – it would have taken you four days in all. You liked to read in bed, so you made a start that evening. Next morning I asked: 'Well, what did you think of the first sixty?' You giggled and nodded and went on nodding so fiercely, trying not to laugh out loud, that I feared your head would fall off.

As it happened, you never read the other pages; you died that evening.

Saturday
Readers have every day asked me not to make an end

to these letters, and yet my instinct tells me that after three months they have served their purpose, which was really to talk to myself about you and us. I wonder if you heard a single word of it. At least I have learned how many grieving and bewildered people there are.

VIP Magazine came here last week and took some photographs. In my dozy, head-in-the-sand way, I was actually not aware until it was too late that it was a kind of Irish version of *Hello,* and I was shocked by the colour pictures of myself. The eyes were no longer mine; it was as if the life had been squeezed out of them. I realised that I have been through a mangle over these past weeks and that the letters have been part of it.

So, like I say, we'll speak privately.

Love,
Jack

AFTERWORD

As I write, it is five months exactly since Paule's death, and letters keep coming in. Yesterday, I replied as follows to a lady whose husband died, aged 34, only three weeks ago:

Dear –, It's very strange that, speaking of our respective grief, you say 'I don't know how you feel because I'm not Hugh Leonard, and I wasn't married to Paule'. In the long Preface to my letters to Paule ... you will find: 'People wrote to say they knew how I felt, although they could not possibly, for they were not I, nor had they lost Paule.'

From this, I think you have already begun to learn. Learn what? Wisdom, perhaps. While you desperately long to return to normality, you already sense that 'normality' is gone for ever. Or rather that a new 'normal' is very slowly growing to take its place. Whether you like it or not a new life is forming. Leave it alone; let it take shape.

You are 30; I am 73, so my life is nearly over. If there were justice in heaven, I would have gone before Paule; I was four years older and, unlike her, I didn't 'mind' myself. When I looked in the cupboard at her side of the bed, half of a pharmacy fell out! Her death, in five brutal minutes, was a shock that opened a door to months of hell, and with the weight of nearly 45 years behind it. I am only now beginning to regain sanity so that I can mention her name to others without my eyes filling with tears.

Women can handle grief better than men; I don't mean that in a callous sense; but in most cases their daily life will continue in the same pattern as of old unless they choose to break it. My daughter Danielle lives and works in England; she is grieving, but she is not among the things of home – *this* home, that is – so it has to be easier for her. I find it hard to be alone and impossible to be with someone else for more than, say, a day at a time. But I do feel the new life beginning to grow, to form like a film over a wound. And you will have another life with – and I know the thought is hateful to you – another, very different kind of love in it, and the smile you mention will one day reach your eyes. That isn't advice – discard every pietistic word of it – it's a prophecy.

Write after a time, if you like and if I am still here, and let me know how you are getting on.

And my *Independent* column for 24 September begins with this entry:

'It is my belief, that the lowest and vilest alleys in London do not present a more dreadful record of sin than does the smiling and beautiful countryside.' Thus spake Sherlock Holmes, and the TV series, *Midsomer Murders*, bears it out. This evening, an unseen person swung a well-aimed shovel, and a blonde hoyden bit the churchyard clay; twenty minutes later, the same anonymous do-gooder rammed what looked like poisoned broccoli down the throat of the village bitch-in-residence.

'I bet you're enjoying this!' I said to the empty sofa, and, as in the case of Macbeth, an 'Amen' stuck in my throat. More tears; but there are silver linings. One of my enduring legacies from Paule has been the new friendliness of strangers encountered when I walk abroad. As I keep saying, more people know Tom Fool than Tom Fool knows, and their smiles and greetings have helped make the road easier. Mind, there is, of course, the occasional Whoopi Goldberg among the turf briquettes, if you follow me.

For instance, today a red-faced, white-haired, angry-looking man – it was not yet opening time – shouted after me in Castle Street: 'Are you better?'

I turned and told him: 'I haven't been ill.'

'No, but your wife passed on. Are you over it?'

He all but drooled in his anxiety to see pain.

Further on, I met – could not avoid – a lady whom I knew of an old date, and her eyes brimmed with tears as we drew near. She clutched my hand and asked: 'What is there to say?' It was a good cue-line, for it enabled me to reply 'Nothing', retrieve my mitt and go on my way. The sort she is, she would cry at Laurel and Hardy.

Earlier in the week, I had completed a long – 6,000 words – Preface to the letters to my wife which ran in the *Sunday Independent* paper for fourteen weeks. It was a task undertaken at the behest of the publisher, and it was not a good idea, for its effect on me was to open a wound that had shown the first signs of healing. Writing the thing brought Paule alive again; and with that came the anguish of having to remember that she was dead – I choose not to prettify what happened by saying that she passed on or away or over.

Pain apart, writing the Preface was self-revealing in a way that my newspaper column – which, after all, is only literary skylarking – could never be. And, like others who have lost a friend, lover, critic and champion, all in one and all at once, I fell to wondering what, if any, kind of future I had.

Daring to plan ahead is always asking for a rabbit punch from Providence, but it is sometimes necessary – flights and hotels and cat-sitters tend to get booked up well in advance. Quite deliberately, however, I have let the year 2001 remain a black hole, with no appointments, no fixtures, no plans. I told myself that with Paule gone I had lost all appetite for living and had nothing more to detain me.

It is strange how abhorrent that kind of talk is to religious people. I note that those who profess to believe unquenchably in the bliss of the world to come, have always been most reluctant to go there. I keep thinking of Pope Pius XII, who, with Somerset Maugham, the Aga Khan, the Duke of Windsor and Gloria Swanson, underwent the Niehans rejuvenation treatment of being injected with cells from unborn lambs. However, I wonder if I may not be something of an old cod, for this evening I had dinner in the presence of a certain ebullient businessman and his delightful wife.

I love gossip, and he fed me this and that delicious titbit, about what erstwhile teetotal personage has lately been slurping too much vintage St Julien and making a show of himself, and what lady lawyer has been shedding her briefs. In between, he reminded me that he himself was richer than God and lived in a sumptuous apartment. When he informed me for the third time that, compared with him, Croesus was a piker, I reflected on an old Irish proverb – is there a new one?

– and thought: 'The nearer the heart, the nearer the lips'.

Later, it was raining and a taxi was not to be had, so my new friend most generously offered to drive me home. As we said goodbye, he declared that meeting me had been a pleasure. Then, by way of a Parthian shot, he added: 'And listen, whatever else, you had a great life.'

Well, for all my expectations – hopes, even – of handing in my dinner pail at an early date, that small word 'had' caused me to damn his impudence and sent me to bed in a perfect snit. 'How dare he?' I thought. 'The sauce! Why did he not say RIP and have done with it?' Gladys, wrapped around my neck like a garrotte, purred in agreement.

The tone of this, now that I re-read it, is slick and chirpy; the pain is still there, but it is either concealed or tarted up. Because my Sunday column is entertainment, the emptiness that is at the heart of my life has been turned into a half-joke. Here is a fellow who protests that he has no reason for living and yet takes offence when an acquaintance puts his life in the past tense. You're on the mend, a woman friend said drily when I told her.

In the letters, I wrote about existing at first from day to day and, later, from week to week; and there was a terrible Monday when I wept for ten hours. A new pattern has developed; I feed the cats, water Paule's plants, am too lazy to bother with breakfast, but have lunch at the pub or in town, or else make do with a sandwich and have a proper dinner with friends.

The weeping still comes. It can be triggered by a lady at a dinner table saying, out of the blue 'Oh, I miss Paule's laugh!' or, as happened yesterday, when the vet came to give the cats their annual injection and innocently said 'It's strange to be here without seeing Paule.' The tears do not last long, and it is depression – the 'black dog' – that is most to be feared. It knows no reason or argument. It comes as an uninvited guest, and leaves when it is ready. It brings with it a terrible calm that says 'This is how the world is'. One's sane self looks on, helpless, as the soul sickens and comes near death. It would cost hardly a thought to walk into the sea. After a time – a week perhaps – when the depression ebbs away and is replaced by a 'high', laughter freezes in one's throat and the thought comes that perhaps the same black dog will return as the price one must pay.

If I delude myself into thinking that I am on the mend, it takes little to be reminded that there is not yet a scar or a carapace, but a wound that can bleed again at a touch. What helps to keep me going is a succession of 'treats': a cruise with friends to the eastern Mediterranean; taking Danielle on the opera train to the Wexford Festival in October; having her with me in New York for Christmas and 'blowing the bankroll' on a reunion for the surviving actors from my play *Da* that was on Broadway twenty-two years. Apart from my deep affection for Dan, all else is no more than a carrot to keep this donkey on the move. Excitement and I have become strangers to each other.

Once, before this thing happened, I asked Dan if in

either her life or work she was 'driven' in the obsessive sense. She told me no, rather curtly, as if it were none of my business – like Paule, she kept her thoughts private. I, on the other hand, *was* driven, but the engine stopped with Paule's death.

It took me until now to realise the cause, and it was not grief, but something even more basic. It was simply that out of love or guilt or whatever reason, anything I did of worth was for her alone. The rest was dross.

And now 'Othello's occupations gone' I must learn not only to do without her, but to live and work without her.